HORSE BITS & PIECES

A SUBLIME EQUINE TRIVIA

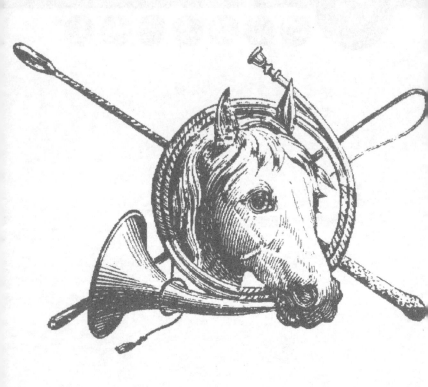

HORSE BITS & PIECES

A SUBLIME EQUINE TRIVIA

SARAH WIDDICOMBE

D&C

David and Charles

A DAVID & CHARLES BOOK
Copyright © David & Charles Limited 2006

David & Charles is an F+W Publications Inc. company
4700 East Galbraith Road
Cincinnati, OH 45236

First published in the UK in 2006

Text copyright © Sarah Widdicombe 2006
Illustrations copyright © David & Charles 2006

Sarah Widdicombe has asserted her right to be identified as author of this work in
accordance with the Copyright, Designs and Patents Act, 1988.

Horse care and riding are not without risk, and while the author and publishers have
made every attempt to offer accurate and reliable information to the best of their
knowledge and belief, it is presented without any guarantee. The author and publishers
therefore disclaim any liability incurred in connection with using the information
contained in this book.

The publisher has endeavoured to contact all contributors of text for permission
to reproduce.

A catalogue record for this book is available from the British Library.

ISBN-13: 978-0-7153-2420-2 hardback
ISBN-10: 0-7153-2420-9 hardback

Printed in Great Britain by CPI Bath Press
for David & Charles
Brunel House   Newton Abbot   Devon

Commissioning Editor Jane Trollope
Editor Jennifer Proverbs
Editorial Assistant Emily Rae
Senior Designer Charly Bailey
Cover design by Emma Sandquest
Production Controller Beverley Richardson
Project Editor Ian Kearey

Visit our website at www.davidandcharles.co.uk

David & Charles books are available from all good bookshops; alternatively you can
contact our Orderline on 0870 9908222 or write to us at FREEPOST EX2 110, D&C
Direct, Newton Abbot, TQ12 4ZZ (no stamp required UK only); US customers call
800-289-0963 and Canadian customers call 800-840-5220.

Welcome to the finest collection of equestrian nonsense the world has ever known. As a discerning selector of books, and a horse person who thirsts after knowledge, you will no doubt have a plan in mind about how you will extract the best from this offering. Perhaps you will start at one end and help yourself to the most tempting snippets, like a horse grazing a pasture. On the other hand, if you are something of an adrenalin-junkie (perhaps you event or barrel race?), you may intend to read it all in a single mind-singeing rush. May I offer this advice:

Like a well-ridden dressage test, this book should be approached with an equal measure of calm and enthusiasm. Try not to rush, use the whole of the arena, and if you lose control and make a fool of yourself in public, remember that horses have been doing that to people for thousands of years.

THE BRUMBY

Australia's feral horse is the descendant of animals brought to the continent by settlers in the 18th and 19th centuries, with only the fittest surviving the arduous journey. One favourite explanation for the origin of the name goes as follows: a James Brumby from Lincolnshire, England, arrived in Australia in 1791. A soldier with the New South Wales Corps and also a farrier, he moved to Tasmania in 1804 and apparently left some horses in New South Wales. When asked who owned them, locals replied 'They're Brumby's'.

-SURVIVOR-

A horse of Morgan breeding named Comanche is remembered as the only US Army survivor of Custer's Last Stand. General George Armstrong Custer and all his men were killed in the famous Battle of the Little Bighorn (a Montana river, called the Greasy Grass by Native Americans) against Lakota, Cheyenne and Arapaho warriors on 25 June 1876.

When reinforcements arrived, they found Comanche wounded but alive. He had been the mount of one of General Custer's officers, Captain Myles Keogh. The horse became the regimental mascot and something of a living legend, brought out for parades and other public occasions. After his death, Comanche was stuffed and put on display in the Natural History Museum at the University of Kansas.

Most Jockey Wins

* The record for the most wins in a year is held by Kent Desormeaux (USA), who notched 598 wins from 2,312 rides in 1989.

* Laffit Pincay Jr (USA) holds the record for career wins, with a total of 9,531 clocked up from 16 May 1964 to 1 March 2003. He retired aged 56, following a serious fall at Santa Anita, California, in which he broke his neck.

COWBOY WISDOM

Don't squat with your spurs on.

POLO SAYINGS

A polo handicap is a person's ticket to the world.
Sir Winston Churchill

Let other people play other things – the king of game is still the game of kings.
Verse inscribed on a stone tablet next to a polo ground in Gilgit, Pakistan

No one ever gets out of polo.
Gonzalo Pieres, former 10-goal player

The Ball no question makes of Ayes and Noes,
But Right or Left as strikes the player goes;
And He that toss'd thee down into the Field,
He knows about it all – He knows – He knows!
From *The Rubaiyat of Omar Khayyam*, translated by Edward Fitzgerald

BETTING JARGON

Where known, the country of origin is shown in brackets, although use of a term may not be restricted to one location.

Note that Sportsbook (USA) = Bookmaker/bookie (UK), and Bettor (USA) = Punter (UK)

Ajax (UK) Betting tax. Also known as Bees, Beeswax.

Beard (USA) Friend, acquaintance or other contact who places bets so that the bookmakers do not know the identity of the actual bettor.

Bees, Beeswax (UK) Betting tax. Also known as Ajax.

Bridge-jumper (USA) Bettor who specializes in large bets on odds-on favourites.

Buy the rack (USA) Purchase every possible daily-double or other combination ticket.

Full cover All the doubles, trebles and accumulators involved in a given number of selections.

Jolly (UK) Bookmaker's slang for favourite.

Juice Bookmaker's commission. Also known as Vig, Vigorish.

Kite (UK) Cheque.

Lock (USA) Almost certain/easy winner.

Picks Betting selections, usually by an expert.

Springer, Steamer Horse whose odds shorten dramatically during the course of betting.

Store (USA) Sportsbook/bookie.

Thick 'un Big bet.

True odds Real odds of something happening, as opposed to what the bookmakers offer.

Vig, Vigorish (Yiddish slang) Bookmaker's commission. Also known as Juice.

Welch, Welsh Fail to pay a gambling bet.

COMMON SAYINGS
* Straight from the horse's mouth.
* Shutting the stable door after the horse has bolted.
* Don't put the cart before the horse.
* Horses for courses.
* Thinking on the hoof.
* Don't look a gift horse in the mouth.

HIGH STANDARDS

The Standardbred horse is the supreme harness racer, whether trotting (legs moving in diagonal pairs) or pacing (legs moving in lateral pairs). The breed took its name in 1879, when a speed 'standard' over one mile was set for entry into the register.

The Standardbred breed traces to Messenger, an English Thoroughbred with Norfolk Trotter influence, imported into America in 1788. His descendant Hambletonian 10, the acknowledged foundation sire of the breed, was foaled in 1849 and between 1851 and 1875 sired over 1,300 offspring – 90 per cent of all modern American Standardbreds trace to him directly, and a premier race of each season is named the Hambletonian.

Current winning times average 1 minute 55 seconds for trotting and 5 seconds less for pacing.

BUZKASHI

Literally translated as 'goat-grabbing', the ancient and dangerous game of Buzkashi is the national sport of Afghanistan and is followed with great enthusiasm by huge crowds. The rules are unwritten, flimsy and fluid – and they are not always adhered to in local matches – but some general principles can be discerned.

THE BALL A large goat or a small calf, minus the head and the legs below the knee. Over time, the ball (*boz*) may become somewhat sticky, slippery and difficult to handle.

THE PLAYERS Usually 10–12 per team, or as many as show up. These are hard men – in the old days, it was not unknown for a player (*chopendoz*) to be stabbed or killed during a game; even today, riders with broken limbs often remount and carry on playing.

THE HORSES Extremely powerfully built and highly trained to bite, kick, push other attackers out of the way and, above all, to stop for nothing but a fall of their own rider.

THE OBJECT Variations exist, but the basic object of the game is to grab the *boz* and carry it to a scoring area. In a form called Tudabarai, the rider has simply to carry the carcass away from the starting circle in any direction, staying free and clear of the other riders. In Qarajai, the carcass must be carried away and around a pole, then back to drop it in a scoring circle – either the home team's (3 points) or the opposition's (1 point). There are no boundaries to the game, so there may be times when the horsemen disappear from view completely.

THE EQUIPMENT Riders carry a short rawhide whip, which is held between their teeth when it is not being used to slash out at other players and their horses.

FOUL PLAY The *boz* may not be tied to a rider's saddle. A *chopendoz* may not hit his opponent on the hand in order to grab the carcass. No shooting or stabbing is allowed. Apart from that, almost anything goes. Play often continues until the *boz* disintegrates.

HOW TALL WILL HE GROW?

A variety of 'formulae' are used by horse breeders to estimate the eventual height of a youngster. Each relies on the assumption that by the end of the horse's first year, the cannon bone has reached its maximum length.

* The distance from the middle of the knee to the ground is 30 per cent of eventual wither height – this measurement is least affected by how the horse is fed and maintained.

* The length of the head is 36–40 per cent of eventual wither height.

* The distance from the elbow to the ground is 60 per cent of eventual wither height.

* The distance from the elbow to the middle of the fetlock is 50 per cent of eventual wither height.

* The distance from the hock to the ground is 40 per cent of eventual wither height.

WORKING HORSES

In the late 19th century in the USA:

* There were 3.5 million horses working in cities.
* 100,000 horses and mules pulled 18,000 horse cars on 5,600km (3,500 miles) of track.
* In Chicago, 82,000 horses produced 600,000 tons of manure per year.

WINNER TO LOSER

Shergar was a supremely talented flat racehorse. Of his eight races, he won six, earning a total of £436,000. As a three-year-old, he triumphed in the Classic Trial by 10 lengths, the Chester Vase by 12 lengths and the Epsom Derby by 10 lengths – the biggest winning margin ever. Shergar also took the Irish Derby and King George VI and Queen Elizabeth Stakes by four lengths each. When he was retired to stud, 34 syndication shares were sold for £250,000 each.

However, Shergar is most often remembered for a very different reason. On 8 February 1983, a week before the start of his second breeding season, the horse was snatched from the Aga Khan's Ballymany Stud in County Kildare, Ireland. The kidnap made front-page news and the conspiracy theories began, persisting to this day.

There is still no conclusive proof of what happened to Shergar. To add insult to injury, the stud syndicate's insurers refused to pay out, saying that the horse could still be alive or have died after the policy expired.

RECORD CROWDS

Badminton Horse Trials – one of only four élite international 'four-star' three-day events – has taken place in the park of Badminton House, Gloucestershire, each May since 1949*. Cross-country day attracts crowds of up to 250,000, the largest for any paid-entry sports event in the UK.

The event was cancelled in 1966, 1975 and 1987, and downgraded to a one-day-event in 1963, all due to bad weather. Most recently, it was cancelled in 2001 following the outbreak of foot-and-mouth disease.

ICELANDIC FACTS

* There is no Icelandic word for 'pony', so the country's only breed is called the Icelandic Horse, despite standing only 13–14hh.

* In 930, a law was passed by the world's oldest Parliament, the Althing, forbidding the use of outside blood on the Icelandic Horse.

* The first breed society was established in 1904, the same year that the car arrived in Iceland.

* The Icelandic Horse possesses a fifth gait, the *tölt*, that is extremely smooth to ride. A display trick is for the rider to hold a full glass in one hand and the reins in the other, without spilling a drop, as his mount proceeds at full *tölt*.

* The Icelandic Horse comes in more than 40 different colours, with about 100 variations.

* The breed is exceptionally long-lived, on average to 25–30 years old, while horses of 40 or more have been recorded.

* Today there are about 80,000 Icelandic Horses in their home country – which has a human population of 270,000 – and around 100,000 have been exported.

POLO HANDICAPS

Because polo is a difficult game, great discrepancies of skill may exist between players on a team. A handicapping system is for this reason in operation:

* Each player is awarded a handicap rating expressed in goals. These range from –2 goals for beginners, to 10 goals – theoretical perfection. The rating does not reflect the number of goals a player is expected to score in a game.

* The handicaps of each player on the team are added together to provide a team handicap. These handicaps are compared, and the team with the lesser handicap is awarded a goal or goals start.

* About two-thirds of rated players carry a rating of 2 goals or less; few ever advance beyond 3 goals.

* Ratings of 5 goals and above usually belong to professional players.

* Since the inception of the system, fewer than 50 players have been awarded a perfect handicap of 10 goals.

COWBOY WISDOM

If you want to get somewhere, ride one horse at a time.

SOME PHYSICAL FACTS

* Horses cannot breathe through their mouths, and therefore do not pant.

* The average horse's heart weighs around 4kg (9lb).

* Horses cannot vomit.

* With long limbs and large heart and lungs, the horse is designed for galloping. Jumping is not a natural activity for horses – left to their own devices, most will go around obstructions.

RIDING HAT SIZES

Head size (cm)	Riding hat	Jockey skull cap
51	6¼	00
52	6³/₈	00½
53	6½	0
54	6⁵/₈	0½
55	6³/₄	1
56	6⁷/₈	1½
57	7	2
58	7¹/₈	2½
59	7¼	3
60	7¼	3½
61	7½	4
62	7⁵/₈	4½
63	7³/₄	5

STORM CAT
Born 1983 by Storm Bird ex Terlingua by Secretariat

* Storm Cat's is the most expensive stud fee in the world at $500,000 (£265,000).
* Twice leading sire and a record seven times leading juvenile sire.
* Two years in a row, sons of Storm Cat have set September Keeneland sales yearling price records: in 2004, a colt out of Weekend Surprise sold for $8,000,000 (£4,240,000); in 2005 a colt out of Tranquility Lake sold for $9,700,000 (£5,141,000).
* The five most expensive yearling colts ever sold at Keeneland are by Storm Cat, as is the top-selling filly.
* Storm Cat has been the top sire of Keeneland sales yearlings five years in a row (2002–05).
* The highest priced broodmare, sold at the Keeneland November Breeding Stock sale, Cash Run for $7,100,000 (£3,763,000) in 2003,

was in foal to Storm Cat at the time.
* The top-selling weanling, a colt out of Spain for $2,300,000 (£1,219,000) in 2003, was by Storm Cat.
* Storm Cat's book of mares was never filled until his progeny started running: in 2005, he was bred to 109 mares.
* His third crop included Tabasco Cat, who won both the Preakness and the Belmont Stakes.
* Storm Cat's total of 1,184 foals have won more than $94,000,000 (£49,820,000). He has sired 7 champions, 86 graded stakes winners, 138 stakes winners and 86 stakes placers.
* Of his foals of racing age, 54 per cent have won a race and 13 per cent have won a stakes race.
* Progeny have sold for a total of more than $358,000,000 (£189,740,000) at auction.
* More than 120 of Storm Cat's sons have gone on to stud careers of their own; 340 of his daughters have become brood mares, and they have produced 22 more stallions.
* At least 39 different sons of Storm Cat have sired stakes winners.
* Storm Cat has now sired more million-dollar yearlings than any other stallion in history.

WINNER TO LOSER

The equestrian competitions at the Athens Olympics in 2004 provided some extraordinary reversals of fortune.

In showjumping Cian O'Connor (Ireland, individual gold) and Ludger Beerbaum (Germany, team gold) were both disqualified for doping offences, although the FEI judicial committee accepted that neither had intended to enhance the performance of their horse. Rodrigo Pessoa (Brazil) moved up to take the individual gold, while the German team dropped to bronze medal position, leaving the USA to take gold.

In eventing Bettina Hoy (Germany) won, lost, regained (on German appeal) and lost (on French, British and American appeal) her individual and team gold medals, having been penalized for crossing the starting line twice in the final showjumping phase. Leslie Law (UK) was promoted to individual gold, and France took the team competition.

APPALOOSA ORIGINS

The name of these distinctive spotted horses is believed to derive from either the Palouse River, which flows through eastern Washington State and north Idaho, or the tribe named after it. White settlers called the spotted horses of the tribe 'a Palouse horse', which soon became 'Appalousey'. The name Appaloosa was officially adopted in 1938.

BUCKING HORSES

* Around 40 per cent of rodeo bucking horses are in the sport because they have continued to buck off their riders.

* The remaining 60 per cent are bred specifically for the job in programmes that aim to breed back the buck that other horse breeders have tried to reduce or eliminate over time.

* One leading rodeo stock contracting company in the USA estimates that each of their bucking horses works for a grand total of 10 minutes per year.

* This workload leads to exceptional longevity in bucking horses, with many champion broncs in their twenties still bucking off cowboys.

⋄⋄

-SHINIEST BREED-

Revered by Roman emperors and Alexander the Great, Genghis Khan and Marco Polo, the Russian Akhal-Teke breed came originally from the Kara Kum Desert in Turkmenia and takes its name from a tribe, Teke, that lived at the Akhal oasis. This golden-coated horse has influenced many other breeds – the Byerley Turk, one of the three founding sires of the Thoroughbred, may have been an Akhal-Teke – and has often been given to heads of state as a gesture of goodwill. In 1956, Soviet leader Nikita Khrushchev presented HM Queen Elizabeth II with a magnificent stallion called Melekush. His coat displayed the breed's characteristic metallic sheen and the Queen's grooms apparently spent some time trying to wash off this 'polish', but the horse's coat merely glowed more brightly afterwards.

POLO PONIES

Not a breed as such, the ideal polo pony combines speed, intelligence and agility.

Height When the British first came across the game in Persia (now Iran), the ponies used stood 12.2hh. The first height limit in England was 14hh in 1876, then 14.2hh in 1896, until it was abolished in 1919. Polo ponies now average 15.1hh.

England Polo pony breeding has been documented since 1893, the small Thoroughbred Rosewater being regarded as the foundation sire for modern English ponies.

USA Thoroughbreds are often crossed with Quarter Horses to improve agility.

Australia and New Zealand Small Thoroughbreds are used to produce good polo ponies.

Argentina Source of most top ponies since the 1930s, bred by crossing Thoroughbreds with tough little local Criollo horses.

Most important quality 'Heart' – the pony's willingness to give its all, and then some more.

RUMOURED TO BE LAW
In Kentucky, it is illegal for a woman to appear in a bathing suit on a highway unless she is: escorted by at least two police officers; armed with a club; lighter than 90lb (40kg) or heavier than 200lb (90kg). The ordinance specifically exempts female horses from such restrictions.

WORLD'S RICHEST RACING

The Dubai World Cup, held at Nad al Sheba in Dubai in the United Arab Emirates, carries the largest prize fund for a single race: $6 million (£3.3 million), of which $3.6 million (£2.3 million) goes to the winner. In 2000, Godolphin sent out the brilliant Dubai Millennium for the race, so named because they fully expected him to win that year's running, and he duly obliged. In 2002 and 2003, the meeting also boasted the richest day's racing in the world, with a total of $15.25 million (£9.7 million) for seven races, including the Dubai World Cup and the Dubai Kahayla Classic, a race for purebred Arabian horses.

DRESS CODE FOR THE ROYAL ENCLOSURE, ASCOT

Ladies

* Ladies are required to wear formal day dress and a hat that covers the crown of the head.

* Shoulders and midriff must be covered.

* Dresses and skirts should not be more than 5cm (2in) above the knee.

* The late Princess Diana caused a sensation when she appeared bare-legged in the Royal Enclosure, but anyone else would be expected to wear stockings or tights.

* Trouser suits should be full length and of matching material.

Gentlemen

* Gentlemen must wear either black or grey morning dress, including a waistcoat, with a top hat.

* White or brown shoes are frowned upon.

* Military dress may be worn.

* Overseas visitors may wear formal national dress.

THE KIKKULI METHOD

Not all training methods can be improved. Around 1345BCE, Kikkuli, horsemaster to the Hittite King Suppililiuma, wrote the text for a chariot-horse training regime that became an important factor in the Hittites developing their mighty empire. Amazingly, the programme used 'interval training', common in modern training of human athletes, and gave detailed instructions for feeding, work distances/speeds and much more, for a period of almost 200 days. In the early 1990s, endurance rider Ann Nyland, a research student at the University of New England, Australia, duplicated the Kikkuli Method with ten Arabian horses and found that it enabled them to remain sound while becoming extremely fit.

Sample advice: Isolate the stables from the 11th to the 21st day of training, fill any gaps in the walls, windows or doors, and keep the horses indoors. The Kikkuli text does not explain the reason for this, but Nyland's experiment showed it to be an excellent way of weeding out weak horses with respiratory problems.

WHITE HORSE SUPERSTITIONS

* If you see a white dog, you should be silent until you see a white horse.
* Upon encountering a white horse you should spit and make a wish, or cross your fingers until a dog (preferably white) is seen.
* If you lead a white horse through your house it will banish all evil.
* Seeing a white horse on the way to the church is lucky for the bride and groom.
* In some cultures, a white horse is considered a death omen; in others, merely to dream of one signifies death.

SUBLIME HORSES

The Mangalarga Marchador is Brazil's national breed. The horses were originally known as Sublime horses, after the foundation sire from which they were bred. To prove their endurance, in 1994 two Brazilians completed a trail ride of 13,910km (8,694 miles) on Mangalarga Marchador horses. They rode all day and rested at night, and the trip took them 1½ years, using the same horses throughout. The feat was recorded in the *Guinness Book of World Records*.

DONKEY SUPERSTITIONS

* Placing three hairs from a donkey's shoulders in a muslin bag worn around the neck is a cure for whooping cough or measles.

* Sitting backwards on a donkey is a cure for a snakebite or toothache.

* If a woman who is pregnant sees a donkey, the child will be wise and well behaved.

ACCUMULATOR AND COMBINATION BETTING

If successful, an **accumulator** bet is a way of converting a relatively small stake into a large payout, by placing the winnings on one race as the stake on the next race, and so on, for a predetermined number of races. The stake is tied in and any winnings cannot be withdrawn until the last race has been completed, so punters cannot lose their nerve between races. In addition, providing fixed odds are available in advance when the bet is placed, the odds will not reduce as the amount staked increases. The major drawback of a straight accumulator is that any one of the races may not provide a dividend, thereby causing the whole accumulator to fail, regardless of success in the other races.

A **combination** bet offers the possibility of winning big 'accumulator-style' while maintaining a safety net in case one or more bets fail. The initial stake is higher because this is not a single bet but a number of small bets; the chances of losing are therefore reduced, while the chances of walking away with some form of payout remain. The punter places a series of bets on the same races, some of which are single bets, the success of which depends on forecasting any single race correctly; some of which are multiples, the success of which depends on forecasting a specific combination of races correctly; and one of which is the full multiple, the success of which depends on all races being forecast correctly.

COMBINATION BETS

Bet	Singles	Doubles	Trebles	4-folds	5-folds	6-folds	7-folds	8-folds	Total stakes
Straight	1	0	0	0	0	0	0	0	1
2-way	2	1	0	0	0	0	0	0	3
Patent	3	3	1	0	0	0	0	0	7
Trixie	0	3	1	0	0	0	0	0	4
Lucky 15	4	6	4	1	0	0	0	0	15
Yankee	0	6	4	1	0	0	0	0	11
Lucky 31	5	10	10	5	1	0	0	0	31
Super Yankee	0	10	10	5	1	0	0	0	26
Lucky 63	6	15	20	15	6	1	0	0	63
Heinz	0	15	20	15	6	1	0	0	57
Super Heinz	0	21	35	35	21	7	1	0	120
Goliath	0	28	56	70	56	28	8	1	247

OBBY HORSES

The English Hobby Horse dates back to the 16th century, with references to men and boys capering around dressed as tourney horses at masques and pageants. Eventually their popularity waned, and pressure from puritan communities pushed the Hobby Horse tradition to remote parts such as the coastal villages of Minehead and Padstow in the West Country. Other forms, such as the Hooden Horse of Kent and the Mari Llwyd of South Wales, also lingered in isolated communities. Today, a revival of interest in folk activities means that there are probably more Hobby Horses performing in parades and festivals these days than at any other time.

The largest Hobby Horse collection in the world is held by Dan Cavanah (USA), who has amassed 381 items since 1990.

GRAND NATIONAL TRIVIA

* The first Grand National was run on Tuesday, 26 February 1839.

* The largest field was in 1929 with 66 runners – a record number for any horse race. The smallest field was in 1883 with just 10.

* No horse has run in the Grand National more times than Manifesto, who competed eight times between 1895 and 1904. Manifesto won the race twice (1897 and 1899) and finished third three times (1900, 1902 and 1903).

* The greatest number of horses to finish was 23 in 1984. Hallo Dandy, ridden by Neale Doughty, was the winner.

* Trainer Fred Rimell won the National four times with ESB (1956), Nicolaus Silver (1961), Gay Trip (1970) and Rag Trade (1976). Ginger McCain has also won four times but with only two horses: Red Rum (1973, 1974 and 1977) and Amberleigh House (2004).

* Jenny Pitman is the only female trainer to have won the Grand National, with Corbiere (1983) and Royal Athlete (1995). She also finished second with Garrison Savannah (1991) and third with Superior Finish (1996).

* In 1998, Earth Summit became the first winner of the Grand National who was also successful in the Scottish and Welsh Grand Nationals.

* Aintree was the first of the UK's 59 racecourses to go live on the Internet, in October 1995.

* The oldest horse ever to win the Grand National was Peter Simple in 1953 at 15 years old. Why Not (1894) and Sergeant Murphy (1923) were both 13.

* There have been seven long-priced surprises in the last 25 runnings: Last Suspect at 50/1, Royal Athlete and Ben Nevis, both at 40/1, Red Marauder at 33/1, Maori Venture and Little Polveir, both at 28/1, and Rubstic at 25/1.

* Brian Fletcher (1968 Red Alligator, 1973 and 1974 Red Rum) shares a 20th-century record with the legendary Jack Anthony (1911 Glenside, 1915 Ally Sloper, 1920 Troytown), both jockeys having ridden three National winners.

BAREBACK BRONC RULES

* The cowboy must 'mark out' as the horse comes out of the chute, keeping both spurs touching the bronc's shoulders, or he will be disqualified.

* As the bronc bucks, only one of the cowboy's hands may be on the rigging, a leather and rawhide handhold. The other hand must be free and must not touch the horse or the cowboy's own body.

* The rider is also judged on spurring action. In the ideal ride, the cowboy repeatedly draws his heels up from the horse's neck, toes turned outwards, to its withers, near the bareback rigging.

* Most importantly, the rider must stay on. The cowboy is disqualified if he is bucked off before eight seconds have elapsed.

THE QUEEN MOTHER'S WINNERS

The late Queen Elizabeth the Queen Mother was one of National Hunt racing's best-known patrons and owned a total of 461 winners. Her first winner was Monaveen at Fontwell Park on 10 October 1949, and her final success under Rules came courtesy of First Love at Sandown Park on 8 March 2002.

THE EVENTING PHILLIPSES

On 14 November 1973, Princess Anne (later the Princess Royal) married Lieutenant Mark Phillips (later Captain). They had met through their mutual participation in the sport of eventing, and went on to have two children, Peter and Zara, before divorcing in 1992.

Princess Anne won individual gold on Doublet at the European Eventing Championships at Burghley in 1971 and was voted BBC Sports Personality of the Year the same year, aged 21. She won individual and team silver medals in the 1975 European Championships in Germany, and the following year she was a member of the British eventing team at the Montreal Olympic Games.

Mark Phillips won the Badminton Horse Trials in 1971 and 1972, riding Great Ovation, in 1974 on HM The Queen's Columbus, and in 1981 on Lincoln. He won a gold medal with the British eventing team at the Munich Olympic Games in 1972 and a team silver in 1988 at the Seoul Games. Since 1993 he has served as *chef d'équipe* of the United States eventing team.

Zara Phillips won individual and team gold medals on Toytown at the European Eventing Championships at Blenheim in 2005, aged 24; even more impressively, she was a late replacement in the team after another rider had to withdraw. The medals were presented by her mother, whose achievements in the championships she had surpassed.

Peter Phillips is more interested in rugby.

RUMOURED TO BE LAW

In Omega, New Mexico, every woman must 'be found to be wearing a corset' when riding a horse in public. A doctor is required to inspect each woman to make sure that she is complying with the law.

AURAL DISTINCTION

The defining characteristic of the Kathiawari and Marwari horse breeds of India is curling ears that meet at the tips, can turn through 180 degrees, and allow for excellent hearing; this is invaluable in the horses' original role in the battlefield, to warn both horse and rider of impending danger. Today, the Marwari (which can be traced back to 'when the ocean was churned to extract nectar for the gods... a period when horses had wings', according to Shri Mahant Baba Balak Dasji Maharaj, priest and horse breeder) is championed by the Maharajah of Jodhpur, while the Kathiawari is used in traditional games such as tent-pegging and polo, and also as a police horse.

FROM THE EAST

CHUKKA One of the periods into which a polo game is divided. A chukka is seven minutes long, with three minutes between chukkas and a five-minute break at half-time. Games generally comprise six chukkas, but four or eight may also be played. From the Hindustani *chakar* and Sanskrit *cakra*, meaning circle or wheel.

RODEO SUPERSTITION

Don't compete with change in your pocket. It will be all you win. Rodeo life is tough: rodeo cowboys do not receive a salary, and success (and the next entry fee) is entirely dependent on winning.

THREE CLASSIC HORSERACING BOARD GAMES

ESCALADO Chad Valley, 1929
No. of players: 2–6
Playing time: 20 minutes

Popular British tabletop horseracing/betting game. Coloured mechanical horses race across a course vibrated via a handle. The player with the most money after an agreed number of races is the winner.

THE REALLY NASTY HORSERACING GAME Upstarts, 1987
No. of players 2–6
Playing time: 90 minutes

Very interesting game that simulates cheating on the racecourse. Players can bet on another player's horse, and can thus choose to move their own horse badly to help the wagered horse win. Cards also allow players to make a horse fall or force the winning horse to take a drugs test.

TOTOPOLY Waddingtons Games, 1938
No. of players: 2–6
Playing time: 180 minutes

Pioneer of double-sided boards: horses are leased and trained on one side and raced on the other. Players can also own a stable, forage merchant's, veterinary surgery, etc. During training, horses can improve on their original (colour-coded*) chances of winning. Players then back horses on the Tote and the race is run.

* The 12 horses, trained in the Stevedon and Walroy stables, are:

Black	Dark Warrior	Flamenco	Dorigen
Red	Marmaduke Jinks	Leonidas II	Overcoat
Yellow	Play On	Priory Park	Knight Error
Blue	King of Clubs	Jerome Fandor	Elton

Black horses are superior to red, red to yellow, and yellow to blue.

TRIGGER, SMARTEST HORSE IN THE MOVIES

Originally named Golden Cloud, Trigger was purchased by Roy Rogers, King of the Cowboys, in 1938 after he spotted him being ridden by Olivia de Havilland on the set of *The Adventures of Robin Hood*. He reputedly paid $2,500 (£1,365) for the golden palomino wonder horse. From then on Trigger (or, more accurately, several Triggers, some of which were related) appeared in all Rogers' movies, numbering well over 80. The pair also became two of the biggest stars of the early television years, with *The Roy Rogers Show* running on CBS from 1951 to 1964. The show also featured Rogers' wife, Dale Evans, and her own somewhat-less-famous horse, Buttermilk.

When the original Trigger died in 1965, Rogers had the hide stretched over a frame* to stand as a likeness of the rearing horse in the Roy Rogers and Dale Evans Museum. When an investigation revealed that Trigger's meat had been sold to several local 'greasy spoon' diners, butcher John L. Jones was sentenced to five years in prison.

* Contrary to popular belief, the horse was not stuffed.

RUMOURED TO BE LAW
It is illegal to fish from horseback in Washington DC, Colorado and Utah.
Tennessee prohibits riders from lassoing fish.

ROYAL ASCOT WINNERS

HM Queen Elizabeth II's horses have won at Royal Ascot on
a number of occasions:

* On 18 June 1954, Landau won the Rous Memorial Stakes, and
Aureole the Hardwicke Stakes in a notable double.

* The Queen's most successful Ascot races are the Royal Hunt Cup and
the Ribblesdale Stakes, contests she has won three times.

* Her horse Blueprint very aptly won the inaugural running of the
Duke of Edinburgh Stakes (formerly the Bessborough Stakes) in 1999.

* In total, the Queen has enjoyed 19 winners at Royal Ascot.

CHESTNUT ONLY

The Haflinger breed from Austria may appear to be exclusively
palomino, but in fact these striking horses are genetically chestnut
and it is the contrast of their flaxen mane and tail that gives
the palomino impression. The first official record of the modern
Haflinger appeared in 1874, with the foundation stallion 249 Folie.
All modern purebred Haflingers trace back to Folie through seven
stallion lines designated A, B, M, N, S, ST and W.

The Suffolk Punch draught horse is also exclusively chestnut
– note the traditional omission of the 't' when describing the colour
of this breed. The foundation sire of this clean-legged heavy horse,
Crisp's Horse of Ufford, Suffolk, was foaled in 1768, although the
breed was described as early as the 15th century.

URVIVING THE CHARGE OF THE LIGHT BRIGADE

Made famous (or infamous) by Lord Tennyson's eponymous poem, the Charge of the Light Brigade took place on 25 October 1854 as part of the Battle of Balaklava during the Crimean War.

Due to incorrect intelligence, the Brigade suffered heavy losses at the hands of the Russian forces: Lord Cardigan led 673 (some sources state 661) cavalrymen into the surrounded valley, of whom 118 were killed and 127 wounded, and 362 horses were lost.

One lucky survivor was Lieutenant Chamberlayne, who, seated by the side of his dead (favourite) horse Pimento, was passed by Lieutenant Percy Smith. The latter advised Chamberlayne to take off the saddle and bridle and make his way back, as 'another horse you can get, but you will not get another

saddle and bridle so easily'. Accordingly, Chamberlayne placed the saddle on his head and returned along the valley, threading his way through the Cossacks, who were engaged in pillage and killing his comrades. Chamberlayne must have been mistaken for a looter himself, and this probably saved his life.

ON THE RACK

In the 13th and 14th centuries, farmers in northern England bred and trained Fell ponies to be sold to the wealthy as comfortable mounts for long journeys.

In wills, records and inventories of the time, these ponies were usually referred to as 'rakkers' or 'raks', a term that was used loosely to denote riding animals that moved at speed with each foot hitting the ground separately in turn.

Some modern gaited horses, including American Saddlebreds, are still described as performing a 'rack' or 'singlefoot'.

STATE RECOGNITION

The state animal of New Jersey is the horse (*Equus caballus*), so designated in Chapter 173 of the Laws of 1977. Governor Brendan T. Byrne signed the law on 14 August 1977, while attending the farm and horse show at Augusta, Sussex County.

-PROPHET'S THUMBPRINT-

A 'prophet's thumbprint' is a birthmark in the form of an indentation, usually found on the side of a horse's neck. The associated belief is that a horse with such a mark will be outstanding, as it is allegedly a descendant of one of the five brood mares that the Prophet Mohammed particularly treasured and marked with his own thumbprint.

GREY HORSES

Contrary to popular belief, not all grey horses are born black. Grey is not actually a colour in equines, but a pattern superimposed over another, base colour – and this need not be black. A foal of any base colour may turn grey, as long as at least one of its parents is grey. This change can take place rapidly or over a number of years, and appears to correlate loosely with the colour at birth: the darker the foal, the longer the greying process takes.

It is possible to tell whether a foal of a grey parent is going to be grey by looking for white hairs around the eyes – where this is extreme, the foal is said to be 'goggled'; the ears, muzzle, mane and tail may also show some white hairs. Goggled foals tend to lighten in colour more rapidly than other foals.

EXTREME WEIGHT CONTROL

For flat-race jockeys, weight control is a constant battle. 'Wasting' can take many forms: in earlier days, a jockey might put on a rubber suit and bury himself in manure for an extended period, or even swallow the eggs of a tapeworm that would then hatch and eat away at the food in his intestines.

RODEO STATISTICS

* In bareback riding, Wes Stevenson (USA) scored a record 94 points out of a possible 100 on Kelser Rodeo's Cover Girl in Dallas, Texas, in 2002.

* In saddle bronc riding, Doug Vold (USA) scored 95 out of 100 on Transport at Meadow Lake, Saskatchewan, Canada in 1979. This was equalled by Glen O'Neill (Australia) on Franklin's Airwolf at Innisfail, Alberta, Canada in 1996.

* In bull riding, Wade Leslie (USA) scored a perfect 100 on Wolfman Skoal at Central Point, Oregon, in 1991.

* The largest rodeo attendance totals 171,414 over ten performances at the 1991 National Finals Rodeo in Las Vegas, Nevada.

* Top rodeo money-earner is Ty Murray (USA), who competed in saddle bronc, bareback and bull riding for 14 years. He holds records for career earnings ($2,931,227/£1,870,624); annual earnings ($377,358/£240,692); and most prize money won at a single rodeo ($124,821/£79,716) at the National Finals Rodeo in Las Vegas in 1993.

* The record for most rodeos attended is held by James Newland, who attended the Black · Hills Roundup Rodeo for 82 consecutive years after its inception in 1918.

MULTIPLE HITCHES

Many 19th-century American circuses used 40-horse hitches in the street parades that drummed up business for their later performances in tents. The last '40' was seen in 1903 as part of the Barnum & Bailey Circus, but history was recreated when Dick Sparrow drove 40 Belgian draught horses in the 10th anniversary of the Schlitz Circus Parade in Milwaukee, Wisconsin, on 4 July 1972. In 1995, 50,000 spectators at the 50th Navan Fair, Ontario, watched 50 Clydesdales pull a restored freight wagon through the village. More than 738m (2,400ft) of leather were used to make the line that controlled the team, while horses and wagon stretched 44.5m (168ft 6in) from front to back.

RODEO

SUPERSTITION

Never eat peanuts or popcorn in the arena. Eating such foods could cause the cowboy to choke in the middle of a ride or run.

BREEDING MULES

Parent	Male horse (stallion)	Male donkey (jack)
Female horse (mare)	Horse	Mule
Female donkey (jennet)	Hinny	Donkey
Female mule	Horse	Mule
Female hinny	Hinny	Donkey

The mule is easier to breed and usually larger than a hinny. This is because chromosome match-up more often occurs when the jack (male donkey) is the sire and the mare (female horse) is the dam: donkeys have 62 chromosomes, horses 64 and mules 63. Because of this, male mules and hinnies are both sterile, as are almost all female hinnies and mules.

◇◇

ROMAN HORSESHOES

Victorian excavations of the Roman town of Silchester in Hampshire, England, unearthed many everyday objects including an iron 'hippo-sandal' – which bears some resemblance to a slipper – probably used as a temporary shoe for horses crossing stony ground. Its small size is explained by the relatively small stature of Romano-British horses compared to those of today.

◇◇

FRANKIE'S MAGNIFICENT SEVEN

On 29 September 1996, jockey Frankie Dettori rode the winner in all seven races at the Ascot meeting, a feat never achieved before or since. The cumulative odds on his rides amounted to an astronomical 25,095/1.

Dettori's Winners

Cumberland Lodge Stakes	Wall Street 2/1
Racal Diadem Stakes	Diffident 12/1
Queen Elizabeth II Stakes	Mark of Esteem 100/30
Tote Festival Handicap	Decorated Hero 7/1
Rosemary Related Stakes	Fatefully 7/4
Blue Seal Stakes	Lochangel 5/4
Gordon Carter Handicap	Fujiyama Crest 2/1

However, Dettori's remarkable feat still does not match the record set in August 1933 by Sir Gordon Richards, who rode 12 winners in succession. The first came in the last race at Nottingham, followed by all six the next day at Chepstow and the first five the next day at the same track.

Frankie Dettori was crowned English champion jockey in 1994 and 1995. On 29 December 2000, he was awarded an honorary MBE. He was champion jockey again in 2004, and in September of that year, when Ascot Racecourse closed for refurbishment, he was presented with the 'First' position post in acknowledgement of his Magnificent Seven.

TROTTING EXCELLENCE

Norway's Døle breed are harness horses *par excellence*, displaying a superb turbo-charged trot. This feature is jealously guarded and carefully maintained – to the extent that the National Dølehorse Association (established 1967) prohibits breeding from stallions whose legs show defects when X-rayed.

INDONESIAN PONIES

The Sandalwood pony, named after the fragrant wood that is the main export of the Indonesian islands of Sumba and Sumbawa, shows its Arabian ancestry in its good looks, speed and stamina. Sandalwood ponies are raced over distances of 4–5km (2½–3 miles), ridden bareback and wearing a traditional bitless bridle.

In contrast, the Sumba has 'primitive' looks – upright mane, dun colouring, dorsal stripe and zebra leg markings – and is used for lance contests. But this is also Indonesia's prized 'dancing pony': with bells attached to its knees, it dances gracefully to the beat of the drums.

ESTIMATING A HORSE'S WEIGHT

A horse's weight can be estimated using the formula:

$$\text{Weight (kg)} = \frac{\text{girth} \times \text{girth} \times \text{length (cm)}}{11{,}000}$$

Girth = circumference of the horse's body just behind the front legs
Length = length from the horse's point of shoulder to the point of buttocks

RUMOURED TO BE LAW
In Rosario, Argentina, horses are required to wear
hats in hot weather.

HORSE SELLER'S TERMS

Good hack ....Pretty colour.

Flashy .... White socks.

Attractive ....Bay.

Elegant .... Thin.

14.2hh .... 13.3hh.

15.2hh .... 14.3hh.

Should mature to 16.2hh .... Currently 13.2hh, dam is 14.2hh, sire is 15.1hh, every horse in his pedigree for 10 generations is under 15hh – but this horse will definitely defy his DNA.

Arab ....Looks startled.

Thoroughbred .... Looks terrified.

Pony .... Small and hairy.

Warmblood .... Big and hairy.

Cob .... Big and exceedingly hairy.

YOUNG WHACK

In 2001, seven-year-old Young Whack strode to victory in the Racing To Please You Beginners' Steeplechase at Navan, County Meath, Ireland, but subsequently failed a drugs test. The illegal substance detected was... nicotine. Bemused trainer Noel Meade reflected: 'Young Whack will make a hell of a horse when we get him off the fags.'

ROYAL RACING COLOURS

The late **Queen Elizabeth the Queen Mother** inherited her famous blue-and-buff striped colours with black cap and gold tassel from her great-uncle Lord Strathmore, who rode in four Grand Nationals between 1847 and 1850.

HM Queen Elizabeth II's colours are the same as those of Edward VII and George IV as Prince Regent: purple body with gold braid, scarlet sleeves and black velvet cap with gold fringe.

The **Prince of Wales** rode in a number of steeplechases from 4 March 1980 to 21 May 1981, clocking up top-four placings in his first three races. When riding his own horses in these and several less successful races that followed, the Prince wore his own scarlet colours with royal blue sleeves and black cap. His final race was on his grandmother's Upton Grey at Newton Abbot in Devon, where he finished ninth.

-EQUINE APPETITE-
A horse can eat around 2.5 per cent of his own body weight each day.

TRAVELLER

Confederate General Robert E. Lee's favourite horse, the iron-grey Traveller, became a familiar figure among the troops as he carried Lee on the Civil War's many long campaign marches. After the war, Lee took Traveller with him into retirement, and the horse was led behind the hearse when the general died in 1870. Not long afterwards, Traveller stood on a rusty nail and developed tetanus, for which there was no cure. The horse was buried near the Lee Chapel on the campus of Washington and Lee University. In 1907 his remains were disinterred and displayed, before finally being reburied outside the Chapel in 1971.

FROM THE EAST

POLO Ancient eastern game resembling hockey, played on horseback with a long-handled club (mallet) and wooden ball. Introduced first in Calcutta and a little later in Punjab, first played in England in 1871. From Balti (Tibetan dialect in Kashmir) *polo*, Tibetan *pulu*, meaning ball.

FIRST FEMALE JOCKEY (USA)

In February 1969, at the age of 20, Diane Crump became the first female jockey ever to ride in a pari-mutuel race in the USA, at Hialeah Park, Florida. Riding Bridle 'n Bit, she finished 10th out of 12 that day, but went on to record 40 winners in her first season.

In a head-to-head match race in Puerto Rico, Diane's male opponent tried every dirty trick to defeat her, pulling her foot out of the stirrup, holding onto her saddle cloth and pulling at her reins, so (setting sportsmanship aside) Diane did the first thing that came to mind – she cracked him over the head with her whip. Despite winning in the end, the Puerto Rican jockey was booed by the women in the crowd and showered with rotten tomatoes, while Diane was cheered home.

In 1970 Diane Crump became the first woman to ride in the Kentucky Derby; she finished 15th out of 17 runners on the rank outsider Fathom.

HORSE SPEEDS

Walk	5–6.5kmph (3–4mph)
Trot	13–16kmph (8–10mph)
Canter	16–27kmph (10–17mph)
Gallop	average 48kmph (30mph)*

* Thoroughbred racehorse 64kmph (40mph) plus; Quarter Horse 80kmph (50mph) over short distances.

DRESSAGE MARKERS

20 x 40m arena

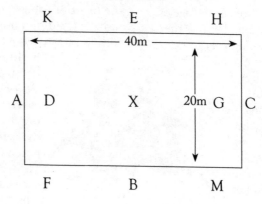

20 x 60m arena

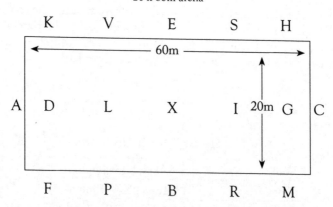

There is no accepted explanation for the order of the letters used as markers in a dressage arena. They seem to have appeared first in the Grand Prix test at the 1932 (or, according to some sources, 1920) Olympic Games, before which letters such as ABCD and XYZ were used. Prior to this the movements were quite different to those seen today, and they were not performed at a fixed letter.

Various theories have been advanced as to the choice of marker letters, such as that they comprise the first letter of the names of cities conquered by the Romans. Perhaps more plausible is the theory that in the Old Imperial German Court the walls of the Royal Mews (stable yard) were apparently marked with letters indicating where each courtier and/or horse was to stand to await the rider:

K	Kaiser/king
F	Fürst/prince
V	Vassal
P	Pferdeknecht/ostler
E	Edeling/Ehrengast/guest of honour
B	Bannerträger/standard bearer
S	Schatzkanzler/Chancellor of the Exchequer
R	Ritter/knight
H	Hofsmarschall/Lord Chancellor
M	Meier/steward

This, of course, offers no explanation for the markers along the centre line.

LUCKY HORSESHOE

■ Nailing a horseshoe above the entrance to the house will bring good luck.

■ Make sure the ends of the shoe point upwards, otherwise the good luck will drain away.

■ Placing the shoe on its side in a C shape may also bring good fortune, as this is symbolic of 'Christ'.

■ A horseshoe nail bent into a circle has the same beneficial effect as the horseshoe itself.

■ When horseshoes were first used, people believed that the shoe itself possessed special powers, as when the shoe was fitted the horse felt no pain.

-FOUR HORSEMEN OF THE APOCALYPSE-

The Four Horsemen of the Apocalypse are mentioned in the Bible in Revelation (chapter 6, verses 1–8), which names just one of them: Death. Further interpretation of the Four Horsemen varies:

Horse	Rider represents
White	Antichrist*, False Christ, False Religion or War, Conquest from Without**
Red	War, Destruction or Pestilence, Plague**
Black	Famine, Unfair Trade, Corruption
Pale***	Death, Genocide

* Contrary to popular belief, the Antichrist is not named in Revelation, and the word does not appear in that book.
** Alternative interpretations may be the result of different Bible translations.
*** From the Greek *chloros*, meaning green – the sickly green tinge of the deathly ill or recently dead. Since the literal translation does not automatically carry these connotations in English, the word is rendered 'pale' in most translations.

BEST MATE

The first horse to win the Cheltenham Gold Cup three times since Arkle in the 1960s, the legendary Best Mate was first past the post in 2002, 2003 and 2004. Ruled out of the 2005 race with a broken blood vessel, he made his much-awaited seasonal debut at Exeter on 1 November, but collapsed during the William Hill Haldon Gold Cup and died from a suspected heart attack.

Owner Jim Lewis had hoped the horse could be buried on the Devon racecourse, where he had won three times including his first-ever 'chase, but this was prevented – despite questions being asked about the decision in the House of Commons – by European regulations brought into force following the foot-and-mouth outbreak of 2001. Best Mate was therefore cremated and finally laid to rest on 10 December behind the winning post at Cheltenham, the scene of his greatest triumphs.

SHOWJUMPING TARIFF

Although the sport of 'lepping' had been popular for some years, the first official list of showjumping penalties was not compiled until the British Show Jumping Association (BSJA) was formed in 1925:

REFUSING OR BOLTING AT A FENCE 1ST 2 FAULTS; 2ND 3 FAULTS; 3RD ELIMINATION

FALL OF HORSE, RIDER OR BOTH 4 FAULTS

HORSE TOUCHES FENCE WITHOUT KNOCKING IT DOWN ½ FAULT

HORSE KNOCKS DOWN FENCE WITH FORELIMB(S) 4 FAULTS

HORSE KNOCKS DOWN FENCE WITH HINDLIMB(S) 2 FAULTS

FORELIMB IN WATER JUMP 2 FAULTS

HINDLIMB IN WATER JUMP 1 FAULT

KNOCKING DOWN WATER FENCE ½ FAULT

The higher penalty for hitting a fence with a forelimb is probably a hangover from the hunting field, where a horse would be more likely to tip up than if he hit a fence with a hindlimb.

GRAND NATIONAL FAVOURITES

Just 12 favourites have won the world's most famous steeplechase since the beginning of the 20th century:

Horse	Year	Odds
Drumcree	1903	13/2
Lutteur III	1909	100/9
Jerry M	1912	4/1
Poethlyn	1919	11/4
Sprig	1927	8/1
Freebooter	1950	10/1
Merryman II	1960	13/2
Red Rum	1973	9/1
Grittar	1982	7/1
Rough Quest	1996	7/1
Earth Summit	1998	7/1
Hedgehunter	2005	7/1

ARE FEWER SPOTS BETTER?

When breeding Appaloosa (spotted) horses, the 'few-spot leopard' pattern – all-over white, very few spots and perhaps darker markings on the legs – is the one to look for. Despite its un-Appaloosa-like appearance, a horse with these markings will produce spotted offspring every time, regardless of the colour of its mate. The downside? All few-spot horses are believed to be night-blind to a greater or lesser extent.

EARLY GAIT ANALYSIS

Before Eadweard Muybridge made his series of famous still photographs in the 1870s, several crude methods were used to try to analyse the way horses move.

- In the 17th century, observers simply watched the horse's legs and listened to the sounds made by the hooves striking the ground, but their conclusions were not accurate.

- Later studies fixed different bells to each of the legs, or shoes that left a distinctive track for each foot. Results were better but still not wholly accurate.

- In the 19th century, French scientist E. J. Marey fixed rubber balls under the horse's hooves which were squeezed as the hoof touched the ground, expelling air up a tube leading from the ball to a lever on a paper recorder carried by the rider.

  He established the sequence of footfalls at each gait, but did not know for how long each foot was in contact with the ground. He concluded – incorrectly – that horses never have three or four feet in contact with the ground at normal gaits.

POLO HISTORY

* In 1859 Joseph Sherer, a subaltern in the Indian Army, Captain Robert Stewart and seven tea planters set up the first club of the modern game, the Silchar Polo Club, which played seven-a-side games against the local Manipuris. Rules were formulated in 1863 and included the stipulation that 'It is to be understood that no player shall be under the influence of bhang, ganja or spirituous liquors.'

* In 1869, after reading about the 'new' game in *The Field* magazine, the 10th Hussars at Aldershot attempted an impromptu game on their chargers using walking sticks and billiard balls. The first organized inter-regiment match on an English ground was played on Hounslow Heath later that year between the 10th Hussars and the 9th Lancers. Playing eight a side, the game lasted for 90 minutes.

* Polo was brought to America by newspaper publisher and sports enthusiast James Gordon Bennett in 1876.

RODEO

SUPERSTITION

A saddle bronc rider always puts the right foot in the stirrup first.
This may be a direct link to the modern cowboy from the knights of medieval Europe, passed from the Spanish *caballero* to the *vaquero* (herdsman) and on to the cowboy. The theory is that during a joust a knight would mount on the right-hand side, because the left or 'sinister' side (Latin *sinister* = left) was considered bad or evil.

HORSE POPULATION USA

The American Horse Council census gives a current total of
6,900,000 horses in the USA.

Racing and racehorse breeding 725,000

Showing 1,974,000

Recreation 2,970,000

Other activities (farm and ranch work, rodeo, polo,
police work etc.) 1,262,800

Since records began:

All-time low 6,000,000 (1949)

All-time high 21,500,000 (1915)

HOUSEHOLD CAVALRY

Recruits to the Household Cavalry
(Life Guards, and Blues and Royals)
undergo 14 weeks' training at
Windsor followed by four weeks at
Knightsbridge Barracks, London. At
the end of this, they are expected
to be riding competently enough
for ceremonial duties – with the
majority having started with no
equestrian experience whatsoever.

PULLING POWER

Finland's only horse breed is famed as a multi-purpose equine (sometimes known as the Finnish Universal), with the stud book split into different types. These include a versatile riding and competition horse, a super-fast trotter* and a harness horse capable of pulling heavier loads than many bigger draught types: while the average horse can pull up to 80 per cent of his own body weight, the Finnish can pull around 110 per cent.

*Of an estimated total horse population in Finland of 57,000, two-thirds are trotters. There are approximately 350,000 trotters (all breeds) in Europe as a whole.

GRAND NATIONAL TRIVIA

* The most recent amateur win came in 1990, when journalist Marcus Armytage scored in record time on Mr Frisk. The pair went on to win the Whitbread Cup in the same season.
* Former British Lions rugby union international John Douglas won the Grand National as an owner in 1979. His 10-year-old Rubstic scored at 25/1 to give Scotland its one and only success in the race.
* Golden Miller started the shortest-priced Grand National favourite ever in 1935 at 2/1, but failed to complete the course.
* Only two grey horses have ever won the Grand National: The Lamb (1868 and 1871) and Nicolaus Silver (1961).
* The Irish have enjoyed great success in the race in recent years: Bobbyjo ended a 24-year drought for Irish-trained horses when winning in 1999, followed by Papillon in 2000, Monty's Pass in 2003 and Hedgehunter in 2005.
* Two jockeys still racing at the time of writing have won the Grand National twice: Carl Llewellyn, on Party Politics (1992) and Earth Summit (1998), and Ruby Walsh, on Papillon (2000) and Hedgehunter (2005).
* Fred Winter won the Grand National twice as a jockey, on Sundew (1957) and Kilmore (1962), and twice again as a trainer with Jay Trump (1965) and Anglo (1966).
* Aldaniti came back from career-threatening injury to win the 1981 race, ridden by Bob Champion, who had himself fought back from cancer. The tale inspired the film *Champions*, starring John Hurt.

EQUINE BIRTHDAY

Horses are aged from 1 January, regardless of when they were born. Breeders of Thoroughbreds destined for the racetrack at a relatively young age aim to have foals born as soon after this date as possible – those born later in the year will be at a competitive disadvantage as they will be racing against horses that are more mature.

If a horse's fifth birthday, say, is on 10 May, he is said to be 'rising' five between 1 January and 10 May.

WEIGHTS FOR HORSES

Type	Height		Weight
	hands	cm	kg
Shetland	8–10	81–102	200–225
Small pony	10–12	102–122	225–350
Large pony	13–14	132–142	250–360
Cob	14–15	142–153	275–400
Lightweight riding horse	15–16	153–163	350–500
Heavyweight riding horse	16–17	163–173	450–600
Draught horse	16–18	163–183	550–800

GOLD STICK

This (now ceremonial) office dates from 1678, when two officers were placed close to the British Sovereign to protect him or her from danger. The name derives from the staff of office, which has a gold head. The office is held jointly by the Colonels of the Life Guards and the Blues and Royals, Regiments of the Household Cavalry. Currently, the office of Gold Stick is held by HRH The Princess Royal (Blues and Royals) and General the Lord Guthrie of Craigiebank (Life Guards), one of whom is on duty at any one time as Gold Stick in Waiting. There are also a Silver Stick and a Silver Stick in Waiting.

PACK-CARRYING CAPACITY

Species	Load	Distance covered per seven-hour day
Horse	60kg (132lb)	39.2km (24½ miles)
Donkey	54kg (119lb)	39.2km (24½ miles)
Mule	181kg (398lb)	46.2km (29 miles)
Elephant	460kg (1,012lb)	24.5km (15½ miles)

HORSE HEIGHT

Horses and ponies are measured from the ground to the withers, in 'hands'. One hand is equal to 10cm (4in). Originally, horses were measured by the width of a person's hand: by placing one hand on the ground, the other above it and moving the first hand over the second, the horse could be measured.

The term used for height is 'hands high' (hh). Often the height is just over a number of hands, for example 14 hands and 1 inch, and the height is referred to as 14.1hh. Today, small ponies (and increasingly horses) are also measured in centimetres.

hh	cm
10	102
10.2	107
11	112
11.2	117
12	122
12.2	127
13	132
13.2	137
14	142
14.2	148
15	153
15.2	158
16	163

COWBOY WISDOM

Whipping a horse makes him smart... not smarter.

HUMAN–HORSE ANATOMY

The horse stands on his fingertips/tiptoes – or rather, fingertip/tiptoe. In the horse, the five digits of the human hand and foot are reduced to one, with the two on either side shrunk to become the splint bones of the horse's leg. The chestnut (on the inside of the knee and hock) and the ergot (at the point of fetlock) are of similar composition to the hoof wall and may be remnants of two further digits, making five in all.

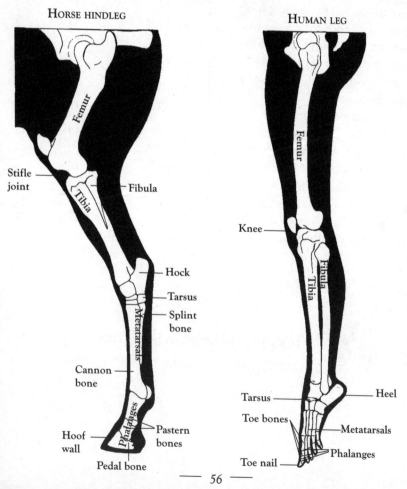

HORSE HINDLEG

Femur

Stifle joint

Tibia — Fibula

Hock

Tarsus

Metatarsals — Splint bone

Cannon bone

Phalanges

Hoof wall — Pastern bones

Pedal bone

HUMAN LEG

Femur

Knee

Fibula
Tibia

Tarsus — Heel

Toe bones

Metatarsals

Toe nail — Phalanges

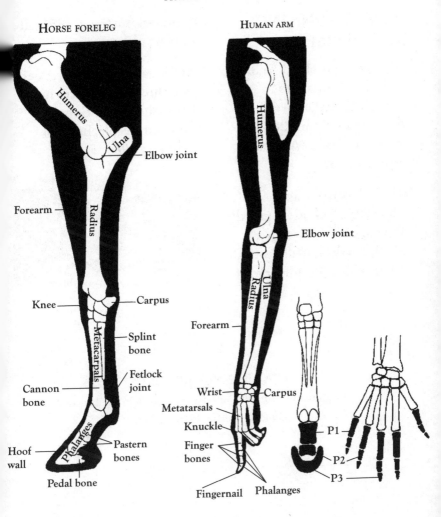

HORSE FORELEG

HUMAN ARM

Humerus
Ulna
Elbow joint
Forearm
Radius
Knee
Carpus
Metacarpals
Splint bone
Cannon bone
Fetlock joint
Phalanges
Hoof wall
Pastern bones
Pedal bone

Humerus
Elbow joint
Ulna
Radius
Forearm
Wrist
Carpus
Metatarsals
Knuckle
Finger bones
Fingernail
Phalanges
P1
P2
P3

OLDEST WINNING RACEHORSES

* Al Jabal, a purebred Arabian, won the Horseshoes Handicap Stakes over 6 furlongs on 9 June 2002 at Barbury Castle, Wiltshire, aged 19 years.

* The oldest winning Thoroughbreds are reputedly Revenge at Shrewsbury, 1790; Marksman at Ashford, Kent, 1826; and Jorrocks at Bathurst, Australia, 1851, all 18 years old.

* At the same age, Wild Aster won three hurdle races in 1919, and Sonny Somers won two steeplechases in February 1980.

FLAT RUNNER RECORD
The record number of runners for a flat race is 58, in the Lincolnshire Handicap on 13 March 1948.

WHITE HORSES I

There are, or have been, at least 24 hill figures depicting horses in the UK. Most are chalk carvings, and 13 are cut into hillsides on the chalk downs of central Wiltshire, with eight still visible. The oldest, over the border in Oxfordshire, dates from around 3,000 years ago and may have some spiritual significance; most of the rest were probably created within the last 300 years. The term used for cutting the chalk horses is 'leucippotomy'. Several other white horses have been created in different ways.

NAME OF WHITE HORSE	LOCATION	DATE	TYPE	COMMENTS
Alton Barnes	Wiltshire	1812	Chalk cutting	In the nearby village of Alton Priors a sarsen stone is carved with a miniature replica of this white horse.
Cherhill/Oldbury	Wiltshire	1780	Chalk cutting	This white horse once had a glass eye made from upturned bottles pressed into the ground. In the 1970s new bottles replaced the lost originals, but were stolen or damaged. The current eye is stone and concrete.
Devizes (old)	Wiltshire	1845	Chalk cutting	Also called the snobs' horse, 'snobs' being the local dialect for shoemakers, who cut the horse. No longer visible.
Devizes (new)	Wiltshire	1999	Chalk cutting	Cut by 200 local people using a plan of the old horse, but reversed to face right – the only white horse in Wiltshire, and one of only four in the UK, to do so.
Hackpen/ Broad Hinton/ Winterbourne Bassett	Wiltshire	1830s	Chalk cutting	On 23 September 2004 the entire horse was weeded and cleaned single-handedly by Bevan Pope.

HORSESHOE PITCHING

The aim of this game is for players to throw horseshoes around a stake, with the horseshoes closest to the stake scoring most points. A court consists of two stakes and two pitchers' platforms, so that contestants play simultaneously and against each other. Games may be played on a singles, doubles or team basis.

PITCHING DISTANCE 12m (40ft) for men, minimum 9m (30ft) for women, juniors, senior men and disabled persons.

SCORING
No score*	0
Points	1 or 2
Ringer**	3
Ringer and point	4
Double ringer	6

*A shoe must be within 15cm (6in) of the stake to score.
**A ringer is declared when a shoe encircles the stake far enough to allow the touching of both heel caulks simultaneously with a straight edge.

DURATION Pitching of 50 shoes, divided into innings, each comprising the pitching of two shoes by each contestant.

Horseshoe pitching records

MOST WORLD CHAMPIONSHIPS
MEN 10 by Ted Allen between 1933 and 1959 (no championships 1936–9).
WOMEN 10 by Vicky Chapelle-Winston between 1956 and 1981.

MOST RINGERS IN WORLD CHAMPIONSHIPS
175 by Glen Henton in 1965.

LONGEST WINNING STREAK IN WORLD CHAMPIONSHIPS
69 games by Fernando Isaias in 1950–2. Broken by Jim Johnson.

HOUSEHOLD CAVALRY DISTINCTIONS

The Life Guards and the Blues and Royals are both Regiments of the Household Cavalry, instantly recognizable by their plumed helmets and black horses, and beloved by tourists visiting London. Ceremony watchers can distinguish the two Regiments at a glance using the following quick reference guide:

Life Guards	Blues and Royals
Red jacket	Blue jacket
White plume	Red plume
Chin chain worn just below lower lip	Chin chain worn beneath chin

DIAGNOSING LAMENESS

* In trot, a sound horse will hold his head more or less level all the time. If the horse is lame, he will nod each time his 'good' foreleg lands on the ground, because this leg is taking extra weight.

* It is possible for a horse to look slightly lame on a foreleg, when in fact the problem lies in the diagonal hindleg. If a horse that is lame on a hindleg is trotted away from you, the hindquarter on the 'good' side will drop when the sound leg hits the ground because that leg is taking extra weight. Lameness in a foreleg does not usually affect the hindquarters.

AMERICAN WINNERS

One of the most famous hunts in America, the Iroquois, in the Bluegrass region of Kentucky, was founded in 1880. It was named after the first American-bred horse to win the Epsom Derby in England, Pierre Lorillard's Iroquois, who captured the race in 1881 along with the St Leger Stakes that same year. Iroquois' dam, Maggie BB, was a phenomenal brood mare who also produced Herald, winner of the Preakness Stakes in 1879, and Panique, victorious in the Belmont Stakes in 1884.

OLDEST FEMALE BRONC RIDER

Born on 2 October 1943, Jan Youren has been competing in bareback bronc riding since 1954 and continues to ride bucking horses, despite having broken most bones in her body at least once. She also competed in rodeo's most dangerous event, bull riding, for 32 years (men have to stay on the bull for eight seconds and may use only one hand to hold on; women must stay on for six seconds and may use both hands). Jan has clocked up five bareback world championships and 13 reserve bull riding championships, and has been inducted into the Hall of Fame of the National Cowgirl Museum (established 1975 in Hereford, Texas, now at Fort Worth), which honours and documents the lives of women who have distinguished themselves while exemplifying the pioneer spirit of the American West.

LETHAL COLOURS

A horse is said to be 'homozygous' for a certain trait when it has inherited the gene for that trait from *both* its parents. Unfortunately, in the case of some coat colours, homozygosity can be lethal:

- A homozygous roan produces an embryo that is apparently unviable and fails to implant or is reabsorbed shortly after conception.

- Overo is a 'broken' or 'coloured' coat pattern, typical of Native American ponies in the West. In its homozygous form it produces the 'lethal white', a white foal with a defective bowel and often other deformities, which dies within hours of birth.

- The 'splashed white' is a relatively rare broken coat pattern that may be lethal in homozygous form, the foetus being aborted after a few months. Even the non-homozygous ('heterozygous') form is not all good news – deafness is an associated characteristic. Blue-eyed overos may also be deaf.

- The few-spot leopard Appaloosa is luckier than these, night-blindness being the only price paid for homozygous status.

FROM THE EAST

JODHPURS Long riding breeches, tight from knee to ankle. Named after the ancient city of Jodhpur in the state of Rajasthan, north India. Men in this state wear trousers akin to riding breeches, hence the name. Late 19th century.

VELKÁ PARDUBICKÁ

The Velká Pardubická is the Czech equivalent of Britain's Grand National.
Run over 6,900m (4¼ miles) and 30 largely natural

jumps, it is notoriously tough – generally around half the starters cross the finishing line. The most difficult fence is the infamous Taxis, fence 4, which includes a ditch from which horses have had to be winched in the past.

The obstacles are so extreme that on the day horses are taken to a test jump; if they refuse twice, or the jockey falls twice, they are disqualified for their own safety.

The last non-Czech winner of the race came in 1995, when Charlie Mann trained and rode It's A Snip to victory.

COWBOY WISDOM Keep a leg on each side and your mind in the middle.

PRATCHETT'S HORSEMEN

The Four Horsemen of the Apocalypse make appearances in Terry Pratchett's Discworld series of books. *Thief of Time* introduces the fifth horseman, Kaos (Chaos), a.k.a. Ronnie Soak, who left before the rest became famous (akin to a fifth Beatle). In Pratchett's novel *Good Omens* (co-authored by Neil Gaiman), the Four Horsemen comprise Death, War (a horse*woman* here), Famine and Pollution (Pestilence having retired in 1936, following the discovery of penicillin).

LONGEVITY

It is widely believed that ponies are more robust and longer-lived than horses, but as far as records go, horses have the edge.

* The oldest horse was Old Billy, foaled in 1760 in Woolston, Lancashire, who died on 27 November 1822, aged 62.
* The oldest pony was Sancho, a Welsh/Arab cross discovered by the Veteran Horse Society in North Pembrokeshire, Wales, who died in August 2003, aged 54.
* Also clocking up 54 years was the oldest donkey, Suzy, from the USA.

MR ED

The television comedy *Mr Ed* ran on the CBS network in the USA from 1961 to 1966. The eponymous star was a talking horse who spoke only to his owner, Wilbur Post, and acted dumb when anyone else was around. This, of course, created many comic situations for Wilbur (played by Alan Young). Mr Ed was played by a horse named Bamboo Harvester, with his voice provided by veteran actor Allan 'Rocky' Lane. Mr Ed is sometimes compared to Francis the Talking Mule, the star of a film series that ran from 1949 to 1956.

HORSE SELLER'S TERMS

Excellent temperament Never been out of his field.

In-hand prospect Bred for beauty, not brains.

Showjumping prospect Looks superb jumping the gate out of his field.

Eventing prospect Big, fast horse.

Dressage prospect Big, slow horse.

Endurance prospect Fast horse that will turn sometimes.

Mounted games prospect Fast horse that will turn when you least expect it.

Lots of potential Under the right circumstances, you might be able to ride him.

He will do it all Bite, kick, buck, rear...

Very brave Even a whip can't force him back.

Top bloodlines He can't do anything, but that's fine because some horse 20 generations back did something.

Unregistered Probably stolen.

Excellent mother Don't even think about going near the foal.

PRESENTING THE ODDS

The way in which bookmakers present odds (probabilities) varies according to location.

For an event with a 1 in 5 probability of occurring (= 0.2 or 20 per cent), the odds are 0.2/(1–0.2) = 0.2/0.8 = 0.25. If you bet 1 at fair odds and the event occurred, you would receive back 4 plus your original 1 stake. This would be presented as follows:

UK bookmaker 4 to 1 against (written 4/1 or 4–1)

European bookmaker 5.0, to include the returned stake

US bookmaker +400, representing the gain from a 100 stake

For an event with a 4 in 5 probability of occurring (= 0.8 or 80 per cent), the odds are 0.8/(1–0.8) = 4. If you bet 4 at fair odds and the event occurred, you would receive back 1 plus your original 4 stake. This would be presented as follows:

UK bookmaker 4 to 1 on (written 1/4 or 1–4)

European bookmaker 1.25, to include the returned stake

US bookmaker –400, representing the stake necessary to gain 100

Never kick a paper cup thrown down at a rodeo.
This may spook a horse.

RODEO

SUPERSTITION

THREE ODD HORSERACING BOARD GAMES

ROYAL STEEPLECHASE Miro Company, France, 1939
No. of players: 2–8
Playing time: 60 minutes
Card-based horseracing board game. Interestingly, several later variants were added, some inspired by the game of Bridge and created by French officers while prisoners of war in Germany in 1941.

WIN, PLACE AND SHOW Avalon Hill, 1966
(Alternative name: Turf)
No. of players: 3–6
Playing time: 120 minutes
Six-race game with many interesting features, including:
* Two swerves on marked squares are allowed per turn (one for apprentice jockeys).
* Each horse has a racing pattern such as slow or fast starter, stayer or fader, represented by numbers that are added to the die throw, so races can vary greatly in speed.
* Expansions to the game published in 1977 allow players to race the greatest horses from 1860 to the 1970s – Man O' War, Seabiscuit, Secretariat, Seattle Slew and Affirmed are all available for purchase.

AND THEY'RE OFF! A Really Useful Game, 1993
No. of players: 2–22
Playing time: 90 minutes
Noteworthy primarily as the brainchild of Andrew Lloyd Webber, musical theatre composer and racehorse owner; Anthony Pye-Jeary, Managing Director of Dewynters Agency, which handled the global branding of Lloyd Webber's *Cats*; and Charlie Brooks, ex-racehorse trainer (arrested with others in 1999 amid race-fixing allegations, but cleared of all charges), columnist and author of *Crossing the Line*, in which he lifts the lid on the world of racing.

BURMESE

The official birthday of the British Sovereign is marked each year by the military parade known as Trooping the Colour, which takes place on Horse Guards Parade, Whitehall. Over 1,400 officers and men, 400 musicians and 200 horses take part. In 1969, HM Queen Elizabeth II rode her new horse Burmese at the parade, and continued to do so for the next 17 years. After this, rather than have another charger trained for the task, she decided to be driven in a phaeton which had been built for Queen Victoria in 1842.

Burmese, a black mare born at the Royal Canadian Mounted Police ranch at Fort Walsh, Saskatchewan, in 1962, had been presented to the Queen by the RCMP in 1969 when they came to England to perform at the Royal Windsor Horse Show. The mare retired to Windsor in 1986 and died in 1990. In 2005, the Queen unveiled a statue of herself mounted on Burmese, which had been commissioned to commemorate her Golden Jubilee and stands outside the Saskatchewan Legislature.

THE NATIONAL PITMANS

The Pitman family has a special and unique association with the Grand National.

* Having led for much of the race, jockey **Richard Pitman** on top weight Crisp was beaten close home by the legendary Red Rum for his first victory in 1973.

* In 1983, **Jenny Pitman** (ex-wife of Richard) became the first woman to train a Grand National winner, when Corbiere beat Greasepaint. She won the National again in 1995 with Royal Athlete.

* In 1993, Jenny trained Esha Ness to win 'the race that never was', when the Grand National of that year was declared void due to a second false start.

* **Mark Pitman**, son of Richard and Jenny, was beaten into second place in 1991 in a finish somewhat reminiscent of his father's, when on the run-in Seagram galloped past Garrison Savannah, trained by his mother.

GRASS CONSUMPTION

A horse eats for between 16 and 20 hours per day and can consume 2–3kg (4–6½lb) of grass every hour. For a fully grass-kept horse, this adds up to a total of between 32 and 60kg (70½ and 132¼lb) of grass per day.

FAMOUS POLO PLAYERS

BRITISH ROYAL FAMILY (AND CONNECTIONS)
HRH Prince Philip
HRH Prince Charles
HRH Prince William
HRH Prince Harry
Captain James Hewitt
Major Ronald Ferguson

MUSIC
Steward Copeland (The Police)
Bing Crosby
Mickey Dolenz (The Monkees)
Kenney Jones (The Who)
Bryan Morrison (Wham!)
Mike Rutherford (Genesis)

FILM AND TV
Bill Devane
Walt Disney
Clark Gable
Tommy Lee Jones
Stefanie Powers
Will Rogers
Robert Stack
Sylvester Stallone
Spencer Tracy

FASHION
Jodie Kidd

US POLITICS/MILITARY
Theodore Roosevelt
George S. Patton

FASTEST PANTOMIME HORSE

In an event staged at Harrow School, Middlesex, on 18 August 2005, records were set for the fastest pantomime horse over 100m. The rules stipulated that competitors must remain inside their horse costume for the entire race.

Men Charles Astor (front) and Tristan Williams (rear) 13.51 seconds
Women Samantha Kavanagh (front) and Melissa Archer (rear) 18.13 seconds
Mixed Simon Ringshall (front) and Sara Saha (rear) 18.43 seconds

-EARLY SHOWJUMPING-

■ Before the formalization of penalties, decisions in showjumping were somewhat arbitrary: some judges marked according to the severity of the obstacle, others on style.

■ Prior to 1907 there were no faults for a refusal, although a competitor was sometimes asked to continue to the next obstacle for the sake of the spectators.

■ Competitions could continue for as many rounds as the judges saw fit, and often competitors with the least knockdowns were not even in the winning line-up.

■ A water jump would often have drained dry by the time the last competitors jumped it.

■ High jump competitions took place over a single pole set at 1.5m (5ft) to start, but this format was soon abandoned as many horses made the decision to duck beneath it. This probably provided the impetus for the development of 'fillers'.

PURE PERCHERON

To perpetuate the purity of this renowned draught breed, only horses bred at La Perche in Normandy, France, are eligible for entry into the Percheron stud book. Horses bred outside this area – to which the Percheron's original Arabian ancestors were brought and abandoned by invading Moors defeated at the Battle of Tours in 732 – must be entered into a separate register.

FIRST RACING COLOURS

On 4 October 1762, the 19 Stewards of the Jockey Club announced a resolution to register specific racing colours to members 'For the greater Conveniency of distinguishing the Horses in Running, as also for the Prevention of Disputes, arising from not knowing the Colours worn by each Rider'. In the first list of colours registered following the resolution, 18 owners shared 17 sets of colours.

Duke of Cumberland	Purple	Earl of March Mr Vernon	White
Duke of Grafton	Sky blue	Earl of Northumberland	Deep yellow
Duke of Devonshire	Straw	Earl of Gower	Blue with blue cap
Duke of Kingston	Crimson	Viscount Bolingbroke	Black
Duke of Ancaster	Buff	Sir John Moore	Darkest green
Duke of Bridgewater	Garter blue	Mr Grevile	Brown trimmed yellow
Marquis of Rockingham	Green	Mr Shafto	Pink
Earl of Waldegrave	Deep red	Lord Grosvenor	Orange
Earl of Orford	Purple and white	Sir J. Lowther	None

FROM THE EAST

GYMKHANA Local public event consisting of competitions in various sports, especially horseriding, now most commonly used to describe mounted games. In India under British rule, the term denoted an athletics meeting or a public place providing athletics facilities. From the Hindustani *gend-khana*, meaning racket-court (*gend* ball, *khana* court, place), the word was remodelled on the English *gymnasium* in the 19th century.

 COWBOY WISDOM Always drink upstream of the herd.

CHESTNUT SENSITIVITIY

Chestnut horses (particularly mares) are regarded by many as especially sensitive and difficult, being extremely touchy about grooming, saddling, veterinary procedures and so on. Could this be related in any way to the research finding that people with red hair require about 20 per cent more anaesthesia to obtain satisfactory sedation, and are likely to experience more pain from most stimuli?

UNICORNS

THE POPULAR image of the legendary unicorn is of a white horse with a single, usually spiral, horn (the alicorn) that has magical properties. The traditional unicorn, however, has a goat's beard, lion's tail and cloven hoofs, making it more realistic, since only cloven-hooved animals have horns. The unicorn appears in Greek and Roman natural history, not myth, since writers were convinced that it existed. Candidates include:

INDIAN ASS Pliny described this as 'a very ferocious beast, similar in the rest of its body to a horse, with the head of a deer, the feet of an elephant, the tail of a boar, a deep, bellowing voice, and a single black horn, two cubits in length, standing out in the middle of its forehead.'

RHINOCEROS The 13th-century traveller Marco Polo claimed to have seen a unicorn in Java, although his description is clearly of a rhinoceros. However, classical authors distinguished between rhinoceros and unicorn.

ORYX Plausible in appearance from a distance, although the 'horn' projects backwards and, again, classical authors distinguished oryx from unicorns.

NARWHAL Museum relics decorated with supposed unicorn horns actually sport the spiral tusks of this Arctic whale, presumably traded by unscrupulous northern mariners as genuine unicorn horns.

SURVIVAL

Dating back to before the 13th century, horses from the Kiso region of Japan were bred primarily as warhorses. However, because of the small stature of the Kiso, pure breeding was discouraged in later centuries, and during World War II the government demanded that all Kiso stallions be castrated. But for the Japanese belief in keeping a sacred white horse at certain shrines, the Kiso would have died out completely – one was found at a Shinto shrine which, being a holy horse, had not been gelded. All modern Kisos trace back to this one horse, but despite the efforts of specialized breeders, only around 100 remain.

HORSE OF THE SEA

Despite their Latin name *Hippocampus*, meaning horse caterpillar, seahorses are actually fish. They live in water, breathe through gills and have a swim bladder. However, they do not have scales or tail fins and are poor swimmers, while possessing a long, snake-like tail, a neck and a snout that points downwards and sucks up food like a vacuum cleaner.

Males and females are territorial and pair up for life: the female transfers her eggs to the male, who self-fertilizes them in his pouch. Gestation takes 14 days to 4 weeks, and the birth can be protracted with contractions continuing for up to 12 hours. Once born, the babies (fry) are completely on their own, and fewer than one in a thousand survives to adulthood. Not many resemblances to horses, then.

ASCOT ORIGINS

It was Queen Anne who first saw the potential for a racecourse on the open heath at Ascot (then East Cote), not far from Windsor Castle. The racecourse was built in 1711 on her orders, and the first race meeting was held on 11 August that year.

The inaugural event was Her Majesty's Plate, worth 100 guineas, which was open to any horse, mare or gelding over the age of six years. (The story is that the prizes were paid for using money from the Secret Service fund.) The seven runners were all hunters and were required to carry a weight of 12 stone. The race consisted of three separate heats, each 4 miles long, so the winner (unfortunately unrecorded) must have been a horse of exceptional stamina.

RODEO SUPERSTITION

Eat a hot dog before the competition.
A true superstition, as there appears to be no logical explanation.

EPSOM DERBY ODDS

* Three winners of this great race have been returned at odds of 100/1: Jeddah in 1989, Signorinetta in 1908 and Aboyeur in 1913.

* The shortest-priced winner was Ladas in 1894 at 2/9.

* The hottest losing favourite was Surefoot, fourth in 1890 at the unusual odds of 40/95.

TOP SPEEDS

	Maximum stride length	Maximum strides per second	Maximum speed[*]
Thoroughbred racehorse	7m (23ft)	2.25	70kmph (44mph)
Cheetah	7m (23ft)	3.5	114kmph (70mph)
Greyhound	5m (16ft)	4	72kmph (45mph)

[*]An élite human sprinter can reach a maximum speed of almost 40kmph (28mph).

TSCHIFFELY'S RIDE

A Swiss-born, Argentine professor, writer and adventurer (and one-time professional footballer and boxer in England), Aimé Félix Tschiffely (1895–1954) is best known for the epic ride he undertook from Buenos Aires to Washington DC in 1925–8. One of his aims was to prove the hardiness and stamina of the Argentinian Criollo horse: both the geldings he used came through the trip successfully and lived on into old age. Tschiffely wrote two books about the ride: *Tschiffely's Ride* (or *The Ride,* or *Southern Cross to Pole Star*) in 1933, and *The Tale of Two Horses* (1949), which recounted the story from the point of view of his horses, Mancho and Gato.

RACING COLOUR FACTS

* Frederick St John, 2nd Viscount Bolingbroke (1732–87), was an early patron of George Stubbs. He owned several famous horses, including Gimcrack, who was painted by Stubbs in the Viscount's black colours, and the great racehorse Highflyer, which had to be sold to clear Bolingbroke's huge gambling debt. Later, his stud fees made a fortune for Tattersalls.

* The black colours passed to the Duke of Grafton and then to the 9th Duke of Hamilton (1740–1819), whose horses racked up a record seven St Leger wins between 1786 and 1814. The next distinguished registrant was John Bowes, who won four Derby races between 1835 and 1853.

* Willam Cavendish (1720–64), 4th Duke of Devonshire and owner of Chatsworth, Derbyshire, chose 'straw' for his colours. It is still registered to the family and is the oldest continuously used colour in racing.

* The famous 'Aske spots' colours (large green spots on white) of the Dundas family (later Earls of Zetland) of Aske Hall, near Richmond, North Yorkshire, were registered for the first time in 1774 by Thomas Dundas (1741–1820).

EARLIEST VET TEXT

The earliest known veterinary text is a cuneiform tablet from the ancient city of Ugarit, in modern-day northwest Syria, dating to the 14th century BCE.

Sample advice: 'If a horse discharges a putrid liquid, grain and bitter almond should be pulverized together, and it should be poured into his nose.'

HOEMAKER'S DERBIES

Legendary jockey Bill (Willie) Shoemaker rode 8,833 winners from 40,350 rides in his 42-year career, including being first past the post in 11 Triple Crown races, but perhaps his two most famous rides came in the Kentucky Derby.

The first of these was in 1957, when he mistook a furlong post for the finish line and blew a sure win with Gallant Man.

The second was aboard 18/1 shot Ferdinand in 1986, at the age of 54, when Shoemaker became the oldest jockey to win the Run for the Roses (named for the garland awarded to the winner).

LIQUID CONSUMPTION
A horse can drink up to 55 litres (12 gallons) of water per day.

HOW MUCH DOES A HORSE CHEW?

Thanks to painstaking research, it is estimated that:

4,600 (number of chews to eat 1kg of hay) ÷ 3,600 (number of chews in 1 hour, approximately 1 per second) = 1.27 hours to eat 1kg (2.2lb) of hay

A 500kg (1,100lb) horse fed ad lib forage will get through about 12.5kg (27.5lb) per day: 1.27 hours x 12.5kg = 16 hours

This means that 60 per cent of a horse's time is occupied by chewing.

Hunting Pink

The origin of the term 'pink' as used to describe the scarlet coat worn by hunt servants is often attributed to a tailor named Pink. However, this may not be the whole (or even part) of the story.

The tailor story first appeared in America early in the 20th century: the colour pink was supposedly named after a tailor who was famed for his hunting wear. Variations on the spelling of his name – Pink, Pinke, Pinque – are quoted by a number of sources, and clothing suppliers in both England and America repeat the story in their advertising literature, but nowhere is any evidence provided of the existence of this master tailor, despite his being a relatively well-documented trade.

There are several other possible explanations for the use of the term 'pink' by the hunting fraternity. These include:

* Most prosaically, after much use a scarlet coat fades to pink; in rain, the dye may wash out to pink.

* In the early 19th century, 'pink' was used to mean a fashionable dandy, and this may have been transferred to the hunting field.

* Alternatively, the term may have been transferred from its meaning of pinnacle or excellence, as in 'the pink of health'.

* 'Pink' was used as a shibboleth – a social class marker – which may explain its persistence in use.

* The tailor Pink story provided an attractive alternative explanation for those unhappy with the accusation that 'pink' was used as a shibboleth.

* Tailor Pink may have existed as a character in a novel or play. In Victorian humorous writing, giving characters an occupational surname (such as Trollope's Dr Filgrave) was common practice, and at some point people forgot that the famous tailor was, indeed, fictional.

TALLEST HORSE

The tallest living horse is Goliath, a black Percheron gelding born in 1995 and standing 19.1hh (1.95m). Pedigree name Prince Jordan of Lakeview, he is owned by Priefert Manufacturing, Inc., of Texas, who produce ranching equipment. Goliath is one of six horses used to pull a Priefert promotional wagon, and also makes about a hundred personal appearances per year.

On average, Goliath consumes 22.6kg (50lb) of hay and drinks 113.5 litres (30 gallons) of water per day. He eats little grass because he cannot reach it very well: due to his extraordinary height, his neck just isn't long enough for him to graze comfortably. Like a foal, he has to stretch his front legs apart in order to reach down for the grass.

Goliath is, however, still some way short of the all-time record: the tallest horse ever was a Shire gelding called Sampson, foaled in 1846 in the UK. He measured 21.2½hh (2.19m).

THE FISH RACE

The ancestors of the Boulonnais – the 'Thoroughbred' of draught breeds – were the warhorses brought by Julius Caesar's troops to the French coast of Pas-de-Calais on their way to invade Britain. Used for riding, pulling carts and working on the farm, in the 17th century the Boulonnais was also renowned for pulling the wagons that carried the fish catch from the coast to Paris. Today, this latter usage is commemorated biennially in 'La Route du Poisson', a traditional race between teams of harness horses.

-THE POLO FIELD-

* An outdoor polo field is 127m (418ft) long and 27m (90ft) wide, the largest field in organized sport, equivalent to about five soccer pitches.

* The goal posts at each end are 7m (24ft) apart and a minimum of 3m (10ft) high.

* Penalty lines are marked at 27m (90ft) from the goal, 36.5m (120ft), 55m (180ft) and midfield.

* An indoor polo arena for winter play is ideally 91m (300ft) long and 46m (150ft) wide.

* The goal posts at each end are 3m (10ft) apart and 4.5m (15ft) high.

THE CIRCUS MAXIMUS

Chariot racing in Rome dates back to at least the 6th century BCE. Races were held in a *circus*, named for its oval shape. The oldest and largest circus in Rome was the Circus Maximus, built in a valley stretching between two hills, the Aventine and the Palatine. By the time of Augustus, it could seat around 150,000 spectators. The races were extremely popular and played an important political role during the empire in diverting energies that might otherwise have gone into rioting and other types of unrest.

The four Roman racing stables (*factiones*) were known by the colours worn by their charioteers: Red, White, Blue and Green. Fans became fervently attached to one of the factions, although charioteers often moved between them. Winning charioteers and horses could become heroes, but the life expectancy of both was low. Today, little is left of the Circus Maximus except the long, flat shape of the track.

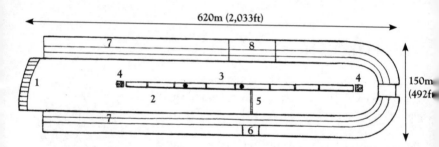

1 CARCERES (STARTING STALLS)

12 staggered, arched openings containing wide stalls, each fronted by a slatted wooden gate, for which charioteers draw lots. An ingenious mechanism opens the gates simultaneously when the emperor or magistrate starts the race by dropping a white cloth (*mappa*).

2 HARENA (TRACK)

The sandy racecourse is about 585m (1,918ft) long and 79m (259ft) wide. The seven laps of a race constitute a total of 5–6.5km (3–4 miles).

3 SPINA (CENTRAL BARRIER)

Rounded off at each end with turning posts, the spina is about 317m (1,039ft) long.
Its high stone walls enclose water channels, statues of the gods, marble shrines and lap counters. In the centre is the huge obelisk brought from Egypt by Augustus.

4 METAE (TURNING POSTS)

High semicircular platforms topped with three tall, conical pillars mark the points where charioteers must try to turn as tightly as possible (leading to many, often fatal, pile-ups). Near the *metae* are lap counters, seven bronze dolphins at one end and seven wooden eggs at the other; one counter is lowered at the completion of each lap.

5 LINEA ALBA (FINISH LINE)

Halfway down the right-hand side of the barrier, a white finishing line extends across the track. In front of the finishing line a temple (6) is built into the stands on the Aventine hill, presided over by deities: the Sun (Sol, whose *quadriga* chariot is pulled by four horses) and the Moon (Luna, whose smaller *biga* is pulled by two).

7 CAVEA (STANDS)

Rows of stone benches several tiers high encircle the track. Corridors beneath the stands, with staircases leading to the seats, are crowded with shops, hawkers and gamblers. The stands are divided according to social class.

8 PULVINAR (IMPERIAL ENCLOSURE)

This resembles a temple rising from the third tier of seats on the Palatine side of the track, directly opposite the finish line. Statues and cult objects of the gods carried in the opening procession are placed here to watch the race. The emperor has a special imperial box within the enclosure.

TONTO'S HORSE

The Lone Ranger TV series (1949–57) was famed for the phrase 'Hi-yo Silver', as the hero's white horse reared spectacularly and his masked rider proceeded to bring wrong-doers to justice. The series starred Clayton Moore as the Masked Man and Jay Silverheels (real name Harold J. Smith) as Tonto, his Native American sidekick, along with Silver – all three characters had retained their names from the original 1930s radio series, but Tonto's horse had a more complex history than most.

In the 1938 *Lone Ranger* film serial, Tonto's horse was called White Feller (Fella/Fellah). In *The Lone Ranger Rides Again* (1939) his name had changed to Scout to match with the radio programme. Scout was played by Sunny, a horse owned by Victor Daniels, who played Tonto.

In the original radio series – first broadcast on 30 January 1933 – Tonto rode double with the Lone Ranger on Silver. After a publicity photo showed the Lone Ranger and Tonto this way, station WXYZ decided to give Tonto his own steed, White Feller. Tonto eventually received Scout in episode 862 of the radio series, broadcast on 5 August 1938, as a gift to replace White Feller. The new horse (as yet unnamed) was presented to Tonto by Chief Thundercloud. In several subsequent shows, Tonto simply referred to him as 'paint horse'.

In episode 874, broadcast on 2 September 1938, the paint horse helped to uncover the leader of a smuggling ring, and there was mention of the horse being 'a sure enough good scout', and Tonto was pleased with this name. In the standard *Lone Ranger* programme closing, the Masked Man hollers 'Hi-yo Silver' and Tonto follows with 'Get 'em up Scout'.

TIC-TAC

Tic-tac sign language is used by bookmakers at British racecourses to indicate movements in the betting price of a horse. They usually wear white gloves and stand on a crate so as to be easily visible. The signs can be encrypted further using the 'twist card', which jumbles the racecard numbers of horses for use by specific firms. Most prices are also known by slang. Some examples are shown.

6/4 Also known as: ear'ole, exes (six in slang), sometimes rouf (four backwards, pronounced 'rofe').

7/4 Also known as: shoulder.

5/2 Also known as: face.

4/1 Also known as: rouf (four backwards, see 6/4).

5/1 Also known as: hand, ching.

10/1 Also known as: net (ten backwards), cockle (sometimes used as slang for £10).

SWIMMING TO MARKET

The herds of feral ponies on the islands of Assateague and Chincoteague off the coast of Virginia and Maryland, USA, are separated by a narrow channel of water; Chincoteague means 'beautiful land across water'. Each July, one of the two herds on Assateague is rounded up by 'saltwater cowboys' and swum across the channel to Chincoteague in front of the cheering spectators. The foals are sold by auction and the remaining horses are swum back to Assateague the next day.

THE TROJAN HORSE

We are all familiar with the story of the Fall of Troy, brought about by 'Greeks bearing gifts' – in this case, a large wooden horse presented as a peace offering following a ten-year siege, but in fact containing soldiers who would bring about the downfall of the city. For a nation that could 'launch a thousand ships' to rescue Helen from Troy, building a wooden structure of this kind would presumably have been no problem – but how large might it actually have been? Reports of the number of warriors contained in the horse vary widely from source to source, from an advance guard of 12 or 13 (Apollodorus) up to a formidable force of as many as 100 (Eustathios). The size of the horse is given as 46m (150ft) long by 15m (50ft) wide (Arktinos) – a truly awe-inspiring structure and an incredible feat of engineering. Assuming this includes the head and neck, an internal body size of, say, 30 x 12m (100 x 40ft) would easily hold 100 men or more. Scaling down for 12 soldiers gives an internal body size of around 11.5 x 4m (37 x 13ft), and an overall size of about 17 x 4.5m (55 x 15ft) – still enough to impress the Trojans, and possibly a more credible achievement of engineering.

TOP HORSE FILMS

Film	Released	Box office gross	Production budget	Awards
The Horse Whisperer	15 May 1998	$184,700,000	$60,000,000	Oscar for Best Music, Original Song + another 4 wins, 16 nominations
Seabiscuit	25 July 2003	$148,257,488	$86,000,000	Nominated for 7 Oscars + another 4 wins, 31 nominations
Hidalgo	5 March 2004	$107,336,658	$100,000,000	2 nominations

EARLY STIRRUPS

The earliest form of stirrups may be those depicted in sculptures in India dating from the late 2nd century BCE. These took the form of a loose surcingle or saddle-strap behind which the rider's feet were tucked. Later depictions from various countries show a stirrup consisting simply of a ring for the rider's big toe. These were used in warmer regions where riders went barefoot, and were clearly impractical in colder climes. Such a design would have no chance of passing health and safety regulations today.

RUMOURED TO BE LAW
In South Carolina, it is legal for adult males to discharge firearms when approaching an intersection in a non-horse vehicle to warn oncoming horse traffic.

SECRETARIAT

A son of Bold Ruler out of Somethingroyal, by Princequillo, the legendary Secretariat was foaled in 1970. The colt won seven of his nine races as a two-year-old and was unanimously voted Horse of the Year. As a three-year-old, he won 9 of his 12 starts, including:

KENTUCKY DERBY Set a record time and ran each quarter mile faster than the previous one, a feat never before achieved in a 1¼-mile race.

PREAKNESS STAKES His winning time may also have been a record, but the timing was disputed and did not stand.

BELMONT STAKES Again beat the record time for the 1½ miles, bettered his Derby time over 1¼ miles and won the race by 31 lengths, another all-time record.

Secretariat was the first horse to win the Triple Crown in 25 years. When he died from laminitis at 19, the autopsy by Dr Thomas Swerczek, a professor of veterinary science at the University of Kentucky, provided a shock: all the horse's vital organs were normal in size except for the heart, which was perfectly healthy yet almost twice the average size, and a third larger than any equine heart Swerczek had ever seen. This may be the explanation for Secretariat's amazing accomplishments.

RUMOURED TO BE LAW

In London, a law in force until 1976 required taxi drivers to carry a bale of hay on top of their cabs to feed their horses.

HIGH JUMP RECORD

The world record for the equestrian high jump, 2.47m (8ft 1in), is held by Captain Alberto Larraguibel Morales (Chile) riding Huaso. The record was set at an official international event at Vina del Mar, Chile, on 5 February 1949, and was ratified by the FEI (Fédération Equestre Internationale) Committee of Records on 28 May 1949.

POLO SHOTS

Forehand Hit the ball forwards or laterally to a team-mate.

Backhand Change the flow of play by sending the ball in the opposite direction.

Neckshot Hit the ball under the horse's neck.

Tailshot Hit the ball behind and under the horse's rump.

EQUINE VITAL SIGNS

Body temperature	37.9 ± 0.5 °C (100.5 ± 1°F)	Over 39.5°C (103°F) indicates a serious problem
Heart rate	38 ± 10 beats per minute	At rest/unstressed*
Respiration rate	12 ± 6 breaths per minute	May be higher in hot weather
Total faeces	17.5 ± 3kg (6½lb) per day	Depends on body weight
Total urine	6 ± 3 litres (5¼ pints) per day	Depends on body weight

* Heart rate at walk is around 80 beats per minute, trotting/cantering 150 beats per minute, galloping up to 250 beats per minute.

NATIVE AMERICAN WARPAINT

Native American warriors painted their horses with symbolic 'medicine paints' made from natural pigments to give them greater courage and strength, intimidate the enemy and display the achievements of horse and rider. A warrior often painted his horse with the same patterns and colours he used for his own body. Horses were painted on both sides, each side telling the same story, with a range of exploit symbols being commonly understood. The colour of these symbols varied from tribe to tribe: for example, the Sioux used red hand prints, the Crow white. In the depiction below, the symbols have been painted on one horse, although this would not have been done in reality.

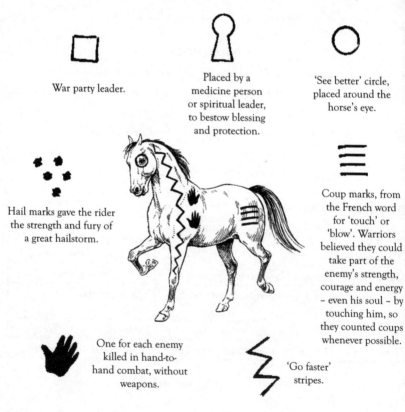

War party leader.

Placed by a medicine person or spiritual leader, to bestow blessing and protection.

'See better' circle, placed around the horse's eye.

Hail marks gave the rider the strength and fury of a great hailstorm.

Coup marks, from the French word for 'touch' or 'blow'. Warriors believed they could take part of the enemy's strength, courage and energy – even his soul – by touching him, so they counted coups whenever possible.

One for each enemy killed in hand-to-hand combat, without weapons.

'Go faster' stripes.

WINNER TO LOSER

Few racing dramas can match the turnaround in fortunes of the late Queen Elizabeth the Queen Mother's horse Devon Loch in the Aintree Grand National of 1956. With only ten horses left in the race, Devon Loch took the final fence well and pulled into a five-length lead over ESB. His jockey, Dick Francis, must have felt certain of victory – until just 36m (120ft) from the winning post, Devon Loch's hindlegs buckled and he went down on his stomach. Francis threw his weight forwards and his mount struggled to his feet, but his hindlegs gave way once again as ESB strode past to win. To make matters worse, Devon Loch might have broken the Grand National record had he finished: ESB was only 0.8 seconds outside it.

Theories as to what had happened are legion: the horse was frightened by the exceptional noise of the crowd, cheering the Queen Mother's horse home; he slipped on a muddy patch of ground; he was put off by the shadow of the water jump to his left; or he simply gave in to cramp and exhaustion.

Devon Loch's jockey retired the following year after a serious fall; but in 1962 Francis published the first of a number of bestselling thrillers based on the racing industry. Loser to winner.

COWBOY WISDOM

A smart ass just don't fit in a saddle.

BUMPER RACING

'Bumper' is an informal term used to describe a flat race specifically for jump horses, in which they gain racing experience before going on to hurdling or chasing. In times past these races were restricted to amateur jockeys, and the name is a description of their sometimes less-than-stylish riding styles.

WHITE HORSE TUNE

In September 2003, the theme tune for children's television series *White Horses* was rated the best ever in *The Penguin Television Companion*. The song, sung by Jacky, had reached number 10 in the UK pop charts in April 1968, the year the series was first shown on BBC1.

Made as a collaboration between RTS (Radio Television Serbia) of Belgrade and BR-TV of Munich, and (badly) dubbed into English, *White Horses* tells the story of 15-year-old Julia, whose uncle Dimitri trains Lipizzaner horses. One of the horses, Boris, is stolen by gypsies who dye his white coat brown so that no one will recognize him. Julia and head groom Hugo set off to find Boris, and when they do a bond is formed between girl and horse, setting the scene for the 12 hour-long adventures that follow.

In the UK, *White Horses* was first shown on Mondays at 5.20pm, after *Blue Peter* or *Jackanory* and before *The Magic Roundabout*. Although the series still exists on film (in Germany), the English soundtrack has long since been lost.

SERIOUS TREKKING

Following historic packhorse trails, coach and stock routes, as well as country roads, the Australian Bicentennial National Trail is the longest horse-trekking trail in the world. The route runs through remote areas from Healesville in Victoria to Cooktown in North Queensland, covering a total distance of 5,330km (3,312 miles).

RECORD UK APPRENTICES

On 5 November 2005 Hayley Turner and Saleem Golam, both 22, made history by sharing the title of champion apprentice jockey – the former as the first woman and the latter as the first Asian to take the title. Already voted Lady Jockey of the Year, Hayley's career total to that point was 102 winners from 1,162 rides, Saleem's 52 winners from 520 rides – he had been laid up for nine months in 2004 following a horrific fall. Each jockey had racked up 44 winners for the season and had failed to increase their total on the last day of the season, despite six rides apiece at Southwell and going head-to-head in the feature race at Doncaster later that afternoon.

ZEBROIDS

All zebra hybrids may be termed zebroids, or zebra hybrids.

Parent	Male zebra	Male horse (stallion)
Female horse (mare)	Zorse	Horse
Female zebra	Zebra	Hebra
Female pony	Zony	Horse or pony
Female donkey (jennet)	Zonkey/zebrass/zedonk	Hinny
Female Shetland pony	Zetland	Horse or pony

The zorse takes the colour (or dominant colour gene) of the mare, and the zebra sire gives it stripes. The same applies to the zonkey: it takes the colour (or dominant colour gene) of the jennet and the stripes of the zebra.

The zonkey is generally more easily bred than the zorse, as donkey and zebra behaviour is more similar than horse and zebra behaviour. Zebra stallions must usually be raised in a special environment to mate with horse mares, while horse stallions usually do not like to mate with zebra mares at all, making the hebra the rarest of the crosses.

BADMINTON WINNERS

The most prolific winner of the Badminton Horse Trials is
LUCINDA GREEN (née Prior-Palmer), who won the event six times
on six different horses:

1973	Be Fair
1976	Wide Awake
1977	George
1979	Killaire
1983	Regal Realm
1984	Beagle Bay

CAPTAIN MARK PHILLIPS won four times on three different horses:
1971 Great Ovation
1972 Great Ovation
1974 Columbus
1981 Lincoln

SHEILA WADDINGTON (née Willcox) is the only rider to have
achieved a consecutive hat-trick:
1957 High and Mighty
1958 High and Mighty
1959 Airs and Graces

Other riders to win three times are:
MARK TODD 1980, 1994, 1996
GINNY LENG (née Holgate) 1985, 1989, 1993
IAN STARK 1986, 1988 (also finished second), 1999
PIPPA FUNNELL 2002, 2003, 2005

-PALOMINOS-

The palomino horse is a colour, not a breed. The ideal is a gold coat – 'between three shades lighter or darker than a newly minted gold coin' – with a pure white mane and tail. In Australia, this colour was originally known as 'sovereign creamy'.

There is no palomino gene as such – the colour is the result of a 'dilution' gene acting on a chestnut base coat. However, the genetics of breeding palominos are well understood and rely on adding the gene carried in double dose by a cremello (blue-eyed cream) horse to the mix:

SIRE AND DAM/COLOUR OF FOAL

palomino x palomino/palomino 50 per cent, chestnut 25 per cent, cremello 25 per cent

palomino x chestnut/palomino 50 per cent, chestnut 50 per cent

palomino x cremello/palomino 50 per cent, cremello 50 per cent

chestnut x cremello/palomino 100 per cent

It has been suggested that the name palomino (meaning 'young pigeon') is derived from that of a Spanish Don, Juan de Palomino, who received a horse of this colour from Hernan Cortès, when the latter set off on his expedition to conquer Mexico in November 1518. Another explanation is that it takes the name of a golden Spanish grape.

BUCEPHALUS

Even as a boy, Alexander had something of 'the Great' about him. Plutarch tells how the lad took on his father Philip's challenge and tamed the wild horse that had been brought to him, by turning its head into the sun to prevent it being frightened by its own shadow. The story may or may not be true, but Alexander certainly rode the horse – which he named Bucephalus (meaning oxhead) because its head was as broad as a bull's – through many battles to create his mighty empire. The horse was eventually killed in battle in 326BCE, and Alexander founded the city of Bucephala (thought to be present-day Jhelum, Pakistan) around the tomb of his steed.

DERBY WINNERS

Lester Piggott is the most successful jockey in the history of the Epsom Derby, having won nine times. His first win came aboard Never Say Die in 1954 and the last 29 years later, on Teenoso. Others who have shone in the big race include:

Sam Arnull	1780 (first-ever Derby), 1782, 1787, 1798
John Arnull (brother of Sam)	1784, 1790, 1796, 1799, 1807
Bill Arnull (son of John)	1804, 1812, 1814
James 'Jem' Robinson	1817, 1836 plus two doubles in 1824/5 and 1827/8
Fred Archer	1877 plus two doubles in 1880/1 and 1885/6
Steve Donoghue	1915, 1917, 1925 plus a hat-trick in 1921/2/3
Willie Carson	1989, 1994 plus a double in 1979/80
Kieron Fallon	1999 plus a double in 2003/4

EADWEARD MUYBRIDGE

Born Edward James Muggeridge in Kingston upon Thames, England, in 1830, the brilliant Muybridge was the most significant contributor to the early study of human and animal locomotion. After moving to the USA, in 1872 Muybridge was hired by railroad baron Leland Stanford to settle a wager: is there a moment in a horse's gallop when all four feet are off the ground? In 1878, Muybridge finally succeeded in taking a sequence of photographs with 12 cameras that captured the moment and gave him instant acclaim. (His experiments had been interrupted in 1874, when he went on trial for the murder of his wife's lover but was acquitted on grounds of justifiable homicide.) In 1882 Stanford published *The Horse in Motion*, with numerous drawings taken from the Muybridge photographs without credit.

Continuing his study of locomotion, in 1879 Muybridge invented the zoopraxiscope, a primitive motion-picture machine. From 1884 to 1887, Muybridge worked at the University of Pennsylvania, Philadelphia, amassing close to 20,000 photographs. The culmination of this was *Animal Locomotion*, which consisted of 781 plates of human and animal movement, put into portfolios and sold by subscription. While these studies certainly appeared scientific, the rediscovery of Muybridge's working proofs shows that he directed, manipulated and selected his photographs to achieve the best prints possible. Unfortunately for Muybridge, only 27 complete portfolios were sold, although many smaller 100-print sets were sold to influential artists and institutions. Eventually, his printer went bankrupt and Muybridge returned to his birthplace, where he died in 1904.

-NAP-

A nap is the selection that racing correspondents and tipsters nominate as their strongest tip of the day or meeting. The term is reputed to stand for Napoleon, borrowed from the card game of the same name. In the bidding in this game, Nap cannot be beaten.

FIRST FEMALE JOCKEY (UK)

In 1804, 22-year-old Alicia Meynell, mistress of Colonel Thornton, competed against Mr Flint in a 4-mile race at York. A reported crowd of 100,000 watched the contest, which was won by Mr Flint. In 1805, riding as Mrs Thornton, she defeated leading jockey Francis Buckle* (with 27 Classic wins to his credit), again at York.

Alicia Meynell's colours, 1804: 'leopard and buff with blue sleeves and cap'.

Mrs Thornton's colours, 1805: 'purple cap and waistcoat, nankeen-coloured skirts, purple shoes and embroidered stockings'.

* Known as the Pocket Hercules, Buckle's name and stature gave rise to a jolly verse in the *Old Sporting Magazine*: 'A Buckle large was formerly the rage, /But now a small one fills our sportive page.'

RODEO
SUPERSTITION

Barrel racers should wear different-coloured socks on each foot.
Supposed to bring luck – but why?

BONE NUMBERS
Most horses have 205 bones in their skeleton; human beings have 206.

WHITE HORSES II

Although the majority of horse figures in the UK have been cut into chalk, some have used other methods.

NAME OF WHITE HORSE	LOCATION	DATE	TYPE	COMMENTS
Westbury	Wiltshire	Early 18th century	Chalk cutting	Recut in 1778, and again in 1873 to its present shape. In the 1950s and again in 1995 the horse was concreted and painted white to reduce maintenance costs.
Uffington	Oxfordshire	Bronze Age, 1200–800BCE	Chalk cutting	This horse faces to the right. Unlike the other white horses, which are solid and naturalistic, this one is formed from stylized curving lines around 3m (10ft) wide. At about 112m (365ft) long, it is over twice as long as the longest of the Wiltshire horses.
Heeley Millennium Park	Sheffield	2000	Concrete painted white	Commemorates Barney, a horse that died following an arson attack at Heeley City Farm in 1995. There is an annual repainting festival, and the appearance of the horse changes each year as a result of this.
Mormond/ Strichen	Aberdeenshire	c. 1800	Filled with white quartz	The only white horse in Scotland. Mormond Hill also has another hill figure, a stag cut in 1870.
Osmington	Dorset	c. 1808	Limestone cutting, whitened with chalk	The only horse with a rider, representing King George III, this horse faces right.

GERVASE MARKHAM (1568–1637)

A prolific writer on country subjects such as hunting, hawking, husbandry, gardening, housewifery and the military, Gervase Markham was best known for his works on horsemanship and the veterinary art. His first book on horses appeared in 1593 under the title *A Discource of Horsmanshipp*, enlarged and reissued with the subtitle *How to chuse, ride, traine, and diet, both hunting-horses and running horses.* This was followed in 1605 by a treatise on *How to trayne and teach horses to amble.*

Markham's major equestrian work came two years later: *Cavelarice, or the English Horseman* bore the modest 'subtitle' *contayning all the Arte of Horsemanship, as much as is necessary for any man to understand, whether he be Horse-breeder, horse-ryder, horse-hunter, horse-runner, horse-ambler, horse-farrier, horse-keeper, Coachman, Smith or Sadler. Together with the discovery of the subtill trade or mistery of horse-coursers, and an explanation of the excellency of a horses understanding, or how to teach them to doe tricks like Bankes his Curtall*: And that horses may be made to drawe drie-foot like a Hound. Secrets before unpublished, and now carefully set down for the profit of this whole Nation.*

In 1610, Markham published his *Maister-peece*, wherein *I have set down every disease,*

and every medicine, so full and so exactly that there is not a farrier in this kingdome, which knowes a medicine for any disease, which is true and good indeed, but I will finde the substance thereof in that booke. Six years later he brought out *Markhams Method: or Epitome*, which he described as containing his *approved remedies for all diseases whatsoever, incident to horses, and they are almost 300, all cured with twelve medicines onely, not of twelve pence cost and to be got commonly everywhere.* This all became too much for those with an interest in selling his existing works, and in 1617 Markham signed a memorandum *That I Gervase Markham of London gent Do promise hereafter Never to write any more book or bookes to be printed, of the Deseases or cures of any Cattle, as Horse, Oxe, Cowe, sheepe, Swine and Goates &c. In witnes whereof I have hereunto sett my hand the 14th Day of Julie.* Nevertheless, in later years he returned to publish *The Complete Farriar, or the Kings High-way to Horsmanship* and *Markhams Faithfull Farrier.*

* A reference to the celebrated performing horse Marocco, which his owner, Bankes, had taught to dance and perform incredible tricks. In *Love's Labour's Lost*, Shakespeare makes reference to Marocco's arithmetical prowess, and there are numerous other allusions to his achievements in contemporary literature. Marocco's most renowned exploit was the ascent of St Paul's Cathedral in 1600.

POLO TRIVIA

- A polo ball can be hit at a speed of 50m/sec (162ft/sec) or 180kmph (112mph).

- The fastest polo ponies can reach a speed of 60kmph (38mph).

- Polo was included in the Olympic Games in 1900 (Paris), 1908 (London), 1920 (Antwerp), 1924 (Paris) and 1936 (Berlin).

- Sir Winston Churchill was a 3-goaler who was part of the 4th Hussars team in India. During his time as Minister of Finance in the early 1920s he played in the team of the British House of Commons.

- One of the most famous polo ponies of all time was Colibri, ridden by Adolfo Cambiaso, who played his final Palermo Open at the age of 19. His rider became the youngest-ever 10-goaler, achieving this handicap also at the age of 19.

- Juan Carlos Harriot is commonly regarded as the best polo player ever.

- The most important polo dynasty is the Heguy family. Throughout the history of the Argentine Open (Palermo Open), Heguys have played with handicaps above 8. Currently, two Heguy teams participate in the Palermo Open every year.

- The Argentine Open in Buenos Aires is considered the World Polo Championship. Only here can you watch teams with a total handicap of 40.

- Qutub-u'd-Din Aibak, founder of the Turkish slave dynasty and builder of one of medieval Delhi's most famous landmarks, the Qutub Minar, reputedly died when he became impaled on the ornate horn of his saddle while playing polo at Lahore in 1206.

- In Tibet, polo supposedly originated in the autumn hunt for the muskrat, which was chased on horseback and beaten to death with a stick. In summer, the riders used a root ball covered with animal skin for practice.

JUMP RACING ORIGINS

- Steeplechasing has its roots in 'pounding matches' held in Ireland in the late 17th century across haphazardly chosen country. The loser was 'pounded' into the ground by being outlasted by the winner, or by falling.

- By the mid-18th century, courses with a landmark winning post, often a church steeple or tower, were more typical, although early versions allowed riders to select their own race route 'from point to point'.

- Many authorities cite a 1752 match in County Cork over 4½ miles from Buttevant Church to the spire of St Leger Church, between Mr Blake and Mr O'Callaghan, as the first of these 'steeplechases'.

- One of the earliest recorded matches in England was in 1790, between Mr Hardy and the Hon. Mr Willoughby for 1,000 guineas, over 9 miles from Melton Mowbray to Dalby Wood. The first reported race involving more than two horses took place in 1792.

- In France, cross-country matches were held in the late 1820s near St Germain, and *courses au clocher* (races to the steeple) started to appear in race programmes in the 1830s.

- The first known steeplechase course (as opposed to a race across country) to be laid out in England was in 1810 at Bedford, a 3-mile course with eight fences 4ft 6in (1.37m) high.

- By the 1840s more than 60 steeplechase meetings were being held regularly in various parts of England.

- In the USA, steeplechasing was introduced by the Washington Jockey Club in a race in Washington, DC in 1834.

- Hurdle races in England date back to at least the early 19th century. It is rumoured that they became popular after George, Prince of Wales, Mrs Fitzherbert and some soldiers raced over sheep hurdles on the downs near Brighton around 1808.

- Point-to-point race meetings began around 1880, over open country with the course route left to each rider. The races were designed for horses that hunted and were ridden by amateurs.

MILKSHAKES

Dishonest trainers and others have been known to administer a 'milkshake' to horses prior to a race. This concoction of baking soda, sugar and water (or sports drink) is passed into the horse's stomach via a tube so that no residue remains in the mouth. It works by increasing blood CO_2 levels, which in turn trigger expulsion of lactic acid from the horse's muscles, blocking pain and fatigue and preventing the horse from tiring in the closing stages of a race.

WHORLS

These circular arrangements of hair growth in the horse's coat are peculiar to each animal and are used as a means of identification. The most obvious and distinctive whorls appear on the forehead and neck. 'Feathering' occurs when the hair lies in a different direction to the normal growth of the coat and may be attached to a whorl.

NAMING THE DERBY

The Epsom Derby was first run in 1780 and was won by Sir Charles Bunbury's horse Diomed – some consolation, perhaps, for his loss of the coin toss between himself and Lord Derby that decided the name of the famous race. Lord Derby's filly Bridget had won the inaugural running of the Oaks the previous year.

NAPOLEON'S HORSE

Napoleon Bonaparte's horse Marengo rose to the height of his fame following the Battle of Waterloo, when he was captured by the British and taken to England. Here, he was displayed both before and after his death, when his skeleton was put on show. There is evidence that the horse – named for Napoleon's success at the Battle of Marengo, north-west Italy, in 1800 – was merely one of a number used by Napoleon through his career, although Marengo is thought to be the mount portrayed in Jacques-Louis David's 1801 painting *Napoleon Bonaparte Crossing the Alps*.

NATURAL SPRINTERS

While horses are born sprinters, with training they are able to achieve distances of over 160km (100 miles) at average speeds of 16–19kmph (10–12mph).

LATIN: EQUUS

English	horse
Welsh	ceffyl
French	le cheval
German	das Pferd
Spanish	el caballo
Italian	il cavallo
Russian	лошадь
Chinese	馬
Icelandic	hestur

-POLO GROUNDS-

♦ The oldest royal polo square is the 16th-century Maidan-Shah, located in Isfahan, Iran.

♦ The highest polo ground is on the Shandur Pass in the North West Province of Pakistan at 3,700m (12,000ft). It is used only during the second week of July for a traditional tournament between teams from Chitral and Gilgit, first played in 1936.

♦ The oldest polo club in existence is the Calcutta Polo Club, founded in 1862.

NORTH AMERICAN EQUINES

The end of the Ice Age signalled the total extinction of many large creatures – including mammoths, mastodons, sabre-toothed tigers and equids – from North America. The latter had existed there for 55 million years, giving rise to new species that crossed land bridges to colonize the Old World, but by 10,000 years ago both the land bridges and the equids of North America were gone. The horse did not return there until 1494, when Christopher Columbus arrived at Hispaniola on his second voyage, bringing with him 24 stallions and 10 mares. The extinct Ice Age equines had been unable to adapt as the climate warmed and forests overtook the open grasslands, while the Old World herds fled, leaving remnants on the open steppes of Central Asia.

Never put your hat on a bed.
This belief may come from the close association of sleep with death, and the dangerous lifestyle of a rodeo cowboy.

RODEO SUPERSTITION

OLYMPIC DRESSAGE WINS

• The record for team gold medals goes to Germany (West Germany 1968–90), with 11, in 1928, 1936, 1964, 1968, 1976, 1984, 1988, 1992, 1996, 2000 and 2004.

• Dr Reiner Klimke won a record six gold medals, taking five team golds between 1964 and 1988 and individual gold in 1984. He also won individual bronze in 1976 for a record seven medals overall.

• Sweden won the team competition in 1948, but were disqualified in favour of France when it was found that team member Genhall Persson, a non-commissioned officer, had been entered as an officer.

FEED WEIGHTS (APPROXIMATE)
Slice of hay = 2kg (4lb 7oz)
Scoop of cubes = 1.5kg (3lb 6oz)
Scoop of concentrate (sweet feed) = 1kg (2lb 4oz)
Double handful of chaff = 250g (10oz)
Slurp of oil = 100g (4oz)

HISTORICAL VALUES

Records of stock purchased by royalty in England during the High Middle Ages include the following equine values:

Late 12th century ....**Foal** 1s

.... **Brood mare** 5s

.... **8 oxen** £1

Early 13th century .... **Mare** 1 mark (13s 4d)

.... **Palfrey** (pacing saddle horse)
2 marks (£1 6s 8d)

.... **Horseshoe and nails** ½d

s = shilling (5p)

d = old penny (½p)

KNIGHT ON HORSEBACK

In October 1704, businesswomen Sarah Kemble Knight set off on an unchaperoned horseback journey from her home in Boston to New York and back again. The trip took five months and Madame Knight, as she was called, kept a detailed diary throughout. On her death in 1727, the diary passed into private hands and lay unknown until 1825, when it was published as *The Journal of Mme Knight*. It is considered to be one of the most authentic chronicles of 18th-century colonial life in America.

THE WINNING EDGE

Stride frequency and stride length both increase as a horse gallops faster. However, it appears to be the ability to get every inch out of a stride that gives a winning racehorse the edge.[*] This is because the less each foot overlaps with the others during the time that each is in contact with the ground, the more each foot's stride can contribute to the total forward distance travelled in one complete stride.

[*] Analysis of the famous 1973 Marlboro Cup Invitational Handicap, which developed into a duel between the legendary Secretariat and Riva Ridge, shows that Secretariat's gallop in the home stretch had an overlap of 18.6 per cent, compared to 24 per cent for Riva Ridge. It was his longer stride that brought the champion victory.

FREESTANDING HORSE

Only the hindlimbs are attached by bone to the rest of the horse's skeleton – the forelegs are attached by muscle and connective tissue alone.

NATURALLY GAITED

Up to the beginning of the 17th century, the majority of horses appear to have been naturally 'gaited', possessing the smooth, running walk that is characteristic of breeds such as the Tennessee Walking Horse today. (In 1605 Gervase Markham published a treatise on *How to trayne and teach horses to amble*.) Trotters, called 'boneshakers', were comparatively uncommon: the ratio in Europe was around 4:1. The development of cities, road-building and travel by horse-drawn carriage, plus the rising popularity of horse racing, changed everything. At the start of the 17th century, it was unusual to find a horse that trotted – and by its end, it was hard to find one that did not.

LONG JUMP RECORD

The world record for the equestrian long jump, 8.40m (27ft 4in), is held by André Ferreira (South Africa) riding Something. The record was set at the national Rend Show in Johannesburg, South Africa, on 26 April 1975, and was ratified by the FEI (Fédération Equestre Internationale) Committee of Records in September 1975.

PONY EXPRESS

Established in April 1860, the Pony Express horseback mail service operated between St Joseph, Missouri, and Sacramento, California, using a continuous relay of riders and horses. The route covered nearly 3,200km (2,000 miles) and pushed man and mount to their limit. Summer deliveries averaged 10 days, winter deliveries 12–16 days, about half the time needed by stagecoach.

The Express clocked up its fastest time ever of 7 days and 17 hours when delivering President Lincoln's Inaugural Address in March 1861. In October that year the first transcontinental telegraph system came into operation, making it possible to transmit messages rapidly from coast to coast. Pioneered by Samuel F.B. Morse, this revolutionary invention brought an end to the Pony Express.

SOME TONY McCOY RECORDS

* A record 74 winners as a conditional National Hunt jockey in 1994.

* Champion jockey ten times from 1995/6 to 2004/5.

* A record 289 winners in one season in 2001/2, surpassing Sir Gordon Richards's total of 269 (set on the flat).

* Fastest jockey to reach 1,000 jump-race winners, breaking Richard Dunwoody's record by six years.

* Broke Dunwoody's record for career winners in 2002 when notching his 1,700th win.

* Dunwoody took 16 years and over 9,300 mounts to reach his milestone; McCoy took half that time, with around 3,000 fewer rides.

FROM THE EAST

NUMNAH Pad placed under a saddle. From Urdu *namdā*, Persian *namad*, meaning felt or carpet. Mid-19th century.

CLOSE RELATIVES

It has been calculated that any two Thoroughbreds picked at random will on average have more than 13 per cent of their genes in common, a degree of relatedness greater on average than that found between half-siblings (12.5 per cent).

TAIL PLAITING

The practice of plaiting a horse's tail for shows may derive from a traditional European custom that it was believed to ward off the attentions of witches. This was apparently more effective if ribbons were woven into the plait – which may have connections with the Crusades, when remnants of the banners taken into battle were plaited into the horse's tail to ward off dark forces.

Never read your horoscope on competition day. Don't tempt fate.

LEFT IS BEST?

IN POLO, THE MALLET MAY ONLY BE HELD IN THE RIGHT HAND. LEFT-HANDED PLAYERS ARE OFTEN THOUGHT TO HIT WITH LESS ACCURACY, BUT GUIDE THEIR PONIES BETTER THAN THEIR RIGHT-HANDED COUNTERPARTS.

HE KING'S TROOP

Established primarily to carry out state ceremonial and routine public duties, the King's Troop has over 100 horses, nearly all imported unbroken from Ireland and trained on by Troop soldiers. In summer, the Troop attends shows both at home and abroad to perform the famous Musical Drive – a spectacular display carried out at a gallop and culminating in the dangerous scissor movement, where teams cross in the centre of the arena with no visible gap between them.

Soldiers and horses that show talent in jumping also compete in civilian competitions, and in the past the Troop has had some notable successes in eventing, including at the Olympics:

1956 Colonel Frank Weldon won Olympic team gold and individual bronze medals on Kilbarry.
1964 Colonel Weldon was *chef d'équipe* of the British Olympic team, which included Captain James Templer and Sergeant Ben Jones, both of the Troop.
1968 Sergeant Jones won an Olympic team gold medal on The Poacher.

POLO RELATIONS

Buzkashi involves two teams of horsemen, a dead goat and few rules. A likely precursor to polo.

Polocrosse is a cross between polo and lacrosse, again played on horseback.

Pato has been played in Argentina for centuries, and may be the reason that Argentines excel at polo.

Elephant polo is exactly as the name suggests. There are two riders per elephant: the *mahout* guides the elephant while the player is responsible for hitting the ball with an extended mallet.

Segway polo is a new version played on Segway HT scooters.

BODILY FLUIDS

A horse's body is 65 per cent water and contains up to 45 litres (10 gallons) of blood. At each beat, the heart pumps around 1 litre (1¾ pints) of blood.

-SPECULATE TO ACCUMULATE-

On 29 September 1996, lucky punter Darren Yates won a total of £550,823.54 ($985,433) from an outlay of just £69.76 ($121.38) (including tax) on a 50p (87c) Super Heinz and £2 ($3.48) each-way accumulator placed on Frankie Dettori's seven winning rides at Ascot. Yates spent 10,000 guineas ($174,000) of his winnings on his own racehorse, which unsurprisingly he called Seventh Heaven. It has yet to win a race.

TWO TYPES OF TRAKEHNER

A trakehner is a cross-country fence consisting of a rail or log over a ditch. The name derives from the Trakehnen area of East Prussia, originally wetlands, which was drained in the 17th and 18th centuries; a programme to breed Trakehner horses was established on the land in 1732. The large, fenced drainage ditches were later used as a test of the three-year-olds' prowess. The take-off was on the downside of the ditch, the landing on the upside, but this style of trakehner fence is no longer seen in eventing, as it is very punishing for the horses. After a horse 'cleared' a trakehner by scrambling under the rail, the rules were changed to require the horse to jump over it.

Horses of the Trakehner breed have won medals in Olympic dressage and eventing, and have so far triumphed in the challenging Pardubická steeplechase a total of nine times in 15 years.

ARABIAN VERTEBRAE

The Arabian breed is renowned for its short back and high tail carriage. These features are due to its having one fewer lumbar vertebra than most other breeds – five instead of six – and 16 tail bones instead of the usual 18.

WHITE FACE MARKINGS

Blaze covers the forehead and front of the face and extends towards the mouth.

Stripe extends down the face and is no wider than the nasal bones. If it is the continuation of a star, it is described as a star and stripe conjoined.

Star is a patch on the forehead. Any description should include size, shape and position.

Few white hairs on the forehead should be described as just that.

White face covers the forehead and front of the face.

Muzzle markings cover both lips and extend to the nostril area.

Snip is an isolated patch of white between the nostrils.

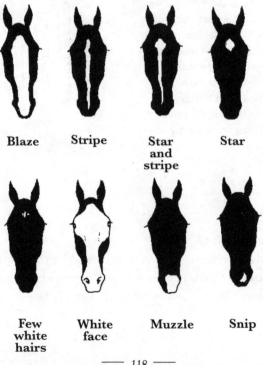

Blaze	Stripe	Star and stripe	Star

Few white hairs	White face	Muzzle	Snip

BAGEL ORIGINS

Legend has it that the first bagel was baked in 1683 by a Jewish baker in honour of King Jan Sobieski of Poland, who had repelled an attempted Turkish invasion of Austria. The king was a great horseman, so the baker fashioned the dough into the shape of a stirrup (*beugal*).

Alternatively, the shape may simply be due to the way the rolls are pressed together on the baking sheet. Whatever its origins, Jewish immigrants brought the bagel to New York in the 1880s, and it eventually became a symbol of the city.

- MARYLAND SUCCESS -

The Maryland Hunt Cup is considered by many to be the toughest jump-race test of horse and rider in the USA. First run in 1894, it comprises 22 solid natural objects, mostly difficult vertical post-and-rail fences, across 4 miles (6.4 km) of undulating terrain.

Two winners of the race, Jay Trump (who won three times, in 1963, 1964 and 1966) and Ben Nevis II (a double winner, in 1977 and 1978), have gone on to win the Aintree Grand National in England.

WHITE LEG MARKINGS

Coronet is situated immediately above the hoof.

Ermine comprises small black or brown marks on white hair surrounding the coronet.

Sock extends from the coronet to just above the fetlock joint.

Stocking takes the white hair to just below the knee or hock.

Pastern covers from below the fetlock joint downwards.

Heel extends from the back of the pastern to the ergot.

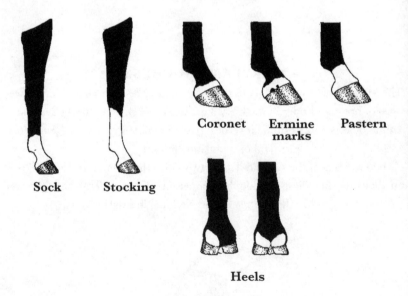

Sock **Stocking**

Coronet **Ermine marks** **Pastern**

Heels

19th-CENTURY ADVICE

Approach the horse firmly, fixing your gaze upon his eye. Have in your hand a six-chambered revolver, loaded with blank cartridges. The moment he attempts to savage you, fire, not point blank at him, but directly in front of his face. This will give the horse a sudden shock and take his attention. If he is in a stall this is your opportunity. Before he has time to recover himself, rush in and seize him by the headstall, and again discharge the revolver close alongside his face, saying: 'What do you mean? How dare you!'

From a 19th-century article *How to Handle a Savage, Vicious Horse*

 COWBOY WISDOM

If you're not makin' dust, you're eatin' it.

HERD SIZE

Wild and feral horse herds consist of relatively few individuals. One in-depth study in the USA found that an average harem comprised a stallion, one to three mares, and their immature offspring. Bachelor groups – of older colts, and stallions without a harem – averaged 1.8, which means that many of these equines were solitary at some time in their lives, although other evidence suggests that a more usual number for a bachelor group is between two and four.

HORSE SELLER'S TERMS

Bold Runaway.

Athletic Runaway, but looks good doing it.

Fantastic movement Bolts.

Well mannered Hasn't stepped on, bitten or kicked anyone for a week.

Professionally trained Hasn't stepped on, bitten or kicked anyone for a month.

Already broken Four fences, one arm, six buckets...

Well started We quit while we were ahead.

Started We quit while we were still alive.

Anyone's ride As long as you have the right protective gear, you'll survive.

Comfortable ride You won't notice he's bucking until you're on the ground.

Needs experienced rider Potentially lethal.

STAY APPARATUS

Equines possess a unique arrangement of tendons and bones that allows their limbs to lock in place while standing. In the forelimbs, the tendons have a groove that locks into the humerus; in the hindlimbs, the patella locks into a crest on the femur. Because of this, horses do not need to expend excess muscular energy in resisting gravity: they actually burn about 10 per cent less energy standing up than lying down. (Sheep and cattle use about 10 per cent more energy standing up than lying down.)

AGEING HORSES

Several early 19th-century British publications dealt with the subject of ageing horses by their teeth, but it wasn't until Australian-born Irish horseman (and ardent self-publicist) Sydney Galvayne travelled through Europe in the 1880s, ageing horses at sales and selling his secret to others, that the practice became widespread. Galvayne's book *Horse Dentition: Showing How to Tell Exactly the Age of a Horse up to Thirty Years*, published around 1885–98, proclaimed the infallibility of his method. However, crooked horse dealers soon developed deceptions such as 'bishoping' (named after a well-known fraudster), which involved drilling an older horse's incisors and burning or dying them to resemble the dark 'cups' found in younger animals. Conversely, a young horse's baby teeth could be removed to make him look up to a year older.

Galvayne's name is still associated with a telltale groove that appears on older horses' teeth. However, it is now accepted that techniques for ageing a horse by its teeth have their limitations.

SOME TOP RACE TIMES

Race	Date	Horse	Jockey	Time	Distance
1,000 Guineas	1994	Las Meninas	John Reid	1 minute 36.71 seconds	1.6km (1 mile)
2,000 Guineas	1994	Mister Baileys	Jason Weaver	1 minute 35.08 seconds	1.6km (1 mile)
Oaks	1975	Juliette Marny	Lester Piggott	2 minutes 29.1 seconds	2.4km (1½ miles)
Epsom Derby	1995	Lammtarra	Walter Swinburn	2 minutes 32.32 seconds	2.4km (1½ miles)
Kentucky Derby	1973	Secretariat	Ron Turcotte	1 minute 59.4 seconds	2km (1¼ miles)
Belmont Stakes	1973	Secretariat	Ron Turcotte	2 minutes 24 seconds	2.4km (1½ miles)
Breeders' Cup Classic	2004	Ghostzapper	Javier Castellano	1 minute 59.02 seconds	2km (1¼ miles)

Note The last three races listed are run on dirt tracks.

-FLORIDA CRACKER-

Originally used for herding cattle in Florida, this breed of agile little horses is named after the cowboys of that state, who were nicknamed 'crackers' because of the sound their whips made. After the Great Depression of the 1930s, cattle were moved to Florida from the Dust Bowl of the Midwest, bringing with them the screw worm parasite. Now, instead of being driven by the cowboys, the cattle had to be roped so they could be treated for the worm – and the Florida Cracker was replaced by the bigger, stronger Quarter Horse. Nevertheless, the breed has survived due to its comfortable, ground-covering gaits.

WINNER TO LOSER

Voted Champion Older Male and Horse of the Year in the USA in 1995 and 1996, Cigar boasted a race record that was truly astonishing.

After a mediocre start to his career, he was switched to racing on dirt and proceeded to win 16 consecutive races, including all 10 starts in 1995, equalling the record of the legendary Triple Crown winner Citation, which had stood since 1950.

Cigar triumphed in two of the richest races in the world, the Breeders' Cup Classic and the Dubai World Cup, and was retired to stud at the end of 1996 with total winnings of $9,999,815.

With his outstanding achievements and superb pedigree – Cigar was a grandson of The Minstrel, himself a son of the great Northern Dancer, while his dam Solar Slew was by the 1977 Triple Crown winner Seattle Slew – hopes were high, but sadly Cigar proved to be infertile.

MEET JOHN S. RAREY

In their introduction to the original 'horse whisperer' Rarey's book *The Complete Horse Tamer*, the publishers frequently place emphasis on matters that seem of less significance today:

One great value of Mr. Rarey's system consists in the fact that it may be taught to, and successfully practised by, persons of little strength – even by boys of fourteen – except where the horse is extremely vicious and powerful... Not only have boys of eighty pounds weight become successful horse-tamers in England, but even English ladies have perfectly subdued and reduced to calmness fiery blood-horses.

John S. Rarey is about thirty years of age, of middle height, and well-proportioned figure, wiry and active rather than muscular – his complexion is almost effeminately fair, with more colour than is usually found in those of his countrymen who live in cities... His walk is remarkably light and springy, yet regular, as he turns round his horse; something between the set-up of a soldier and the light step of a sportsman. Altogether his appearance and manners are eminently gentlemanly.

Rarey (1827–66) became a rich man after he demonstrated his method – in which the horse is laid on the ground using a system of ropes – for Prince Albert and Queen Victoria. He travelled the world teaching his skills: in one demonstration he took four hours to tame a zebra from completely wild to ridden docility. Rarey's method was adopted as the official training procedure of the US Army from 1862. The English magazine *Punch* suggested that the method be practised on obnoxious politicians, and the American *Harper's Weekly* recommended it as a cure for errant husbands.

Never wear yellow in the arena.
The association of the colour yellow with
cowardice probably led to this prohibition.

RODEO

*S*UPERSTITIO*N*

FROUDE NUMBER

Almost all animals, including the horse, change from walk to trot at a Froude number of 1.0, named after engineer, hydrodynamicist and naval architect William Froude (1810–79). This number is the ratio of the centrifugal (inertial) force pulling the animal's centre of mass upwards as it swings over the arc described by the leg, to the gravitational force that is trying to pull it down. As the speed of the walk increases, the centre of mass moves faster and the centrifugal force increases while the gravitational force remains the same. Eventually, the centrifugal force exceeds gravity – the ratio of the two will be greater than 1.0 and the walk will 'lift' off the ground. The horse then moves into a gait that does not remain on the ground for so long and has an airborne phase: the trot.

RUMOURED TO BE LAW
In New York City, it is illegal to open or close an umbrella in the
presence of a horse.

MAKE YOUR OWN HOBBY HORSE

TOURNEY HORSE

This consists of a large plastic hoop or bent wooden-strip frame that fits around the 'rider's' waist and is held in place by braces or a belt. Drape the frame with heavy fabric to conceal the rider's lower body and legs. Make a tail from frayed string. Fix a painted wooden head to a neck of stout cardboard tube, through which controls can be run to open and close the horse's mouth. Dress the top half of the rider as a huntsman, jockey or cavalryman.

MAST HORSE

Make a large horse's head from papier-mâché applied to a chicken-wire framework. Cut holes for eyes and nostrils, and then paint and decorate the head. The space inside can be used to house a battery to operate flashing eyes or other extras. Mount the head on a pole and stitch a blanket in place to conceal the operator's body, and fix a tail to the back.

MASK HORSE

Make a horse's head as above and pad the inside so that it can be fitted safely over the operator's own head. The rest of the costume can either conceal or clothe the horse's human body shape.

THE GATWICK NATIONAL

Since 1839, the Grand National has been held away from Aintree racecourse, Liverpool, on three occasions during World War I. The racecourse had been taken over by the War Office following the 1915 race, and it was decided to move the world's greatest steeplechase to a specially constructed course of the same distance as Aintree at the racecourse that stood from 1891 to 1940 on the site of Gatwick Airport, West Sussex.

* The 1916 race was named the Racecourse Association Steeplechase.
* The 1917 and 1918 races were named the War National Steeplechase.
* The winner of the 1918 race was Poethlyn, ridden by Ernie Piggott, grandfather of legendary flat-race jockey Lester Piggott. Second was Ballymacad, winner of the 1917 race. Poethlyn went on to win the race for a second time in 1919 (making him one of just seven dual Grand National winners), when it was restored to its home at Aintree. Starting at 11/4, he was the shortest-priced winner of the race ever.

GYPSY WISDOM

Gypsy gold does not chink and glitter, it gleams in the sun and neighs in the dark.

CLEVER HANS

Around the turn of the 20th century, a horse known as Clever Hans baffled audiences in Germany with his ability to solve simple mathematical problems (including square roots) and tap out the answers with his hoof. His trainer, Herr von Osten, was convinced Hans was a 'thinking' horse, as were the first investigators (two zoologists, a psychologist, a horse trainer and a circus manager) commissioned by the Berlin Psychological Institute, who could find no sign of fraud and concluded that the horse possessed the mathematical ability of a 14-year-old child.

It was when psychologist Oskar Pfungst took the tests a step further that the truth emerged: Hans could not reach the correct answer to a problem if none of the people present knew the solution. The horse had in fact been 'reading' almost imperceptible cues – a tensing of muscles, changed breathing and heart rates, straightened posture, facial expressions – in the audience as he reached the correct answer, and would duly stop tapping his hoof once these were manifest.

Von Osten was humiliated, the investigators regarded the result as proof that animals cannot think, merely react – and no one at the time stopped to ponder the huge implications for horse training of Clever Hans' remarkable ability to 'read' human beings.

ESTIMATED HORSE POPULATIONS

Worldwide, all equines* 120,000,000

Worldwide, horses only 60–65,000,000

USA 6,900,000 **wild horses** 43,600

Europe 7,200,000

> **UK** 975,000
>
> **Germany** 680,000
>
> **France** 450,000

Australia 1,100,000 **Brumbies** 400,000

Argentina 2,000,000

Mexico 6,000,000 **donkeys** 3,000,000 **mules** 3,000,000

China 12,000,000

Mongolia 3,000,000

*Equine figures include horses (*Equus caballus*), asses (*E. asinus*) and hybrids between the two.

<><><><><><><><><><><><><><><><><><><><><><><><><><><><><><><><>

WHITE SOCKS

Either:
One white foot, buy him.
Two white feet, try him.
Three white feet, be on the sly.
Four white feet, pass him by.

Or:
One white foot, keep him not a day,
Two white feet, send him far away,
Three white feet, sell him to a friend,
Four white feet, keep him to the end.

<><><><><><><><><><><><><><><><><><><><><><><><><><><><><><><><>

THE DISASTROUS NATIONAL

The 1993 Grand National was memorable for all the wrong reasons – particularly as far as the Aintree officials were concerned. Demonstrators at the first fence had caused a slight delay to the race, but the main problems were caused by the starting tape, which managed to get caught around one of the horses as the field set off.

The horses were recalled and the race was restarted, but this time the tape wrapped around jockey Richard Dunwoody and another false start was called – but this time it was too late for most of the field. The flagman stationed 100 yards down the course signalled to the jockeys and nine pulled up before the first fence, but the rest did not see him and carried on with the race.

Officials tried to attract the jockeys' attention as they reached The Chair fence, but were mistaken for protesters. Ten runners stopped after the first circuit, but the rest continued and seven horses eventually finished. Esha Ness, trained by Jenny Pitman, crossed the line first – and it was only then that jockey John White realized his moment of Grand National glory had come in a void race. Despite his huge disappointment, White remained philosophical: 'At the end of the day, racing is something to do in the afternoons. There are more important things in life.'

SHOE OR SHOO?

A 'shoe-in' or, more correctly, 'shoo-in', denotes an easy or sure winner of a horserace (and, by extension, any sporting event). Various explanations for the origins of the phrase are in circulation:

* 'Shoe-in' is a slurred pronunciation for 'sure win'.
* Spelt in this way, the phrase honours legendary jockey Bill Shoemaker, many of whose mounts would have been regarded as certain winners.
* A 'shoo-in' is a racehorse so fast that you can merely shoo it across the finish line, rather than having to urge it on more strongly.

However, the explanation generally accepted as correct is slightly less innocent. Spelt 'shoo-in', the phrase was first used in print in 1928 and originally described a horse expected to win because the race was fixed. The implication was that the horse would win even if its performance was so lacklustre that it simply wandered up to the finish line somehow and had to be 'shooed in' to victory – 'to shoo' meaning to drive a person or animal in a given direction by making gestures or noises, 'shoo' being a sound commonly used.

RUMOURED TO BE LAW

In Guernee, Illinois, it is illegal for women weighing more than 200lb (90kg) to wear shorts while riding horses.

POLO STATISTICS

- Polo is played in more than 60 countries and enjoyed by more than 50 million people each year.

- Argentina have scored the highest number of goals at Federation of International Polo (FIP) World Championship finals with 35, followed by Brazil with 29.

- Six FIP World Championships have been contested since their inception in 1987; Argentina have won three.

- The most chukkas played on one ground in a single day is 43, by the Pony Club on Number 3 Ground at Kirtlington Park, Oxfordshire, on 31 July 1991.

- The record for the highest number of goals scored in an international match has not been broken since 1936, when Argentina beat the USA 21–9 at Meadowbrook, Long Island, New York.

- The total cost for a team to take part in a season of high-goal competition (including the cost of the ponies and their upkeep, stable staff, professional players and travel) is estimated at between £190,000 ($300,000) and £640,000 ($1,000,000).

SOME HORSE FESTIVALS

Festival of Fantasia Held in Meknes, Morocco, since 1977. Thousands of horsemen gather to display their skills.

White Turf racing Horse racing on snow in St Moritz, Switzerland.

Feria de Sevilla Began as a cattle trading fair in Seville, Spain, in 1847, now a round-the-clock spectacle of flamenco, bullfighting and parades featuring horses decorated with flowers.

Luminarias Held on the eve of St Anthony's Day (patron saint of animals) in San Bartolomé de los Pinares, Spain. Horses are ridden through flames in symbolic purification.

Sa Sartiglia Held in Oristano, Sardinia. Comprises a medieval procession and jousting between masked knights.

Oswald von Wolkenstein Ritt Held in the Italian Alps and named after a medieval troubadour of the area. The ride includes challenging mounted games and tournaments.

Ride of the Kings Held in Vlĉnov, Czech Republic, since 1808. Believed to commemorate the escape of the Hungarian King Matthias Corvinus following defeat by the King of Bohemia in 1469, in which he disguised himself by wearing female folk costume. Today the horses are heavily decorated with colourful ribbons, and riders wear traditional dress.

Semana Criolla Takes place during Holy Week in Montevideo, Uruguay. Gauchos take up the challenge of various rodeo events and stage displays of horsemanship.

Litang Festival Held on the Litang plateau in Tibet. Includes a race and demonstrations of spectacular stunts on horseback.

MOTIVATOR

The Royal Ascot Racing Club was formed in 1998, with 229 members, including celebrities such as Sir Andrew Lloyd Webber, Sir Clement Freud, Simon Cowell and Mel Smith. In 2005, the Club's horse Motivator, leased from Ascot Racecourse, won the Epsom Derby, netting each owner £3,000 ($5,220) paid in the form of reduced/free membership. They also receive half of the eventual value of the horse above the £75,000 ($130,500) originally paid (by Ascot Racecourse) for him.

Following a serious leg injury, Motivator was retired in October 2005 and went to stud in 2006 under an agreement that values him at around £4,000,000 ($6,960,000). Motivator raced a total of seven times, winning both starts as a two-year-old, including the Group One Racing Post Trophy at Doncaster, his first three-year-old start in the Dante Stakes at York and the Derby, followed by a second in the Eclipse Stakes and Irish Champion Stakes and fifth in the Prix de l'Arc de Triomphe.

-THE BREATHING HORSE-

At rest, a horse takes around 12 breaths per minute and moves about 5 litres of air in and out of its lungs with each breath, giving a total of around 60 litres per minute at rest. This volume may reach 1,800 litres per minute during full exercise or heavy work.

GRAND NATIONAL FENCES

The Grand National course at Aintree covers 4 miles 856 yards (7.17km) and includes 16 fences, 14 of which are jumped twice, and a run-in totalling 494 yards (449m).

Fence 6/22 Becher's Brook The most famous fence, named after Captain Martin Becher, who rode Conrad in the first Grand National in 1839. The horse ploughed into the fence, catapulting Becher over the top of this drop fence and into the brook. He is reputed to have said he had not known 'how dreadful water tastes without whisky in it'.

Fence 7/23 Foinavon Fence In 1967, a loose horse veered sharply across the face of this relatively straightforward fence and every horse fell, refused or could find nowhere to jump – except for 100/1 outsider Foinavon, who was so far behind that he missed the chaos. His resulting lead of around 40 lengths had been whittled down to 15 at the finishing post by horses that had been re-presented at the now infamous fence.

Fence 8/24 Canal Turn A plain fence, but positioned at a right-angled turn to the left, necessitating an angled jump if lengths are not to be lost. On the first

circuit in 1928, Easter Hero fell here and brought down all but seven of the 42 runners. By halfway only five were left in it, and at the last just two. Billy Barton fell, leaving 100/1 chance Tipperary Tim to come home alone. Billy Barton was remounted to finish second with no other finishers, a record low for the race.

Fence 9/25 Valentine's Brook In 1840, Irish amateur jockey Alan Power bet that he would be leading at halfway on his mount Valentine. He was a furlong clear of the field at the Canal Turn, but as he approached the next fence the horse slowed as if to pull up. At the last moment he changed his mind and produced a spectacular corkscrew-type leap, clearing both fence and brook – which from then on became known as Valentine's Brook.

Fence 15 The Chair The biggest fence in the race: 1.57m (5ft 2in) with a 1.82m (6ft) ditch on the take-off side. The name comes from a seat positioned alongside which was once used by one of the judges.

Fence 16 Water Jump This fence is 83.8cm (2ft 9in) high with 2.89m (9ft 6in) of water on the landing side, but rarely causes problems. Until 1845, it was a stone wall.

FROM THE FRENCH

The lingering association of hunting with the privileged in society may in part date from a time when certain types of quarry were reserved for the monarch and his company. The French Revolution extended hunting rights to that country's commoners, while in England this process occurred as a gradual evolution.

The legacy of the Norman aristocracy's role in the genesis of English hunting may remain in the loss of the final 't' in the pronunciation of 'covert' (from the French couvert, meaning covered) and in the folk etymology of the foxhunting cry 'Tally-ho' from the French 'Il est haut', meaning 'He is up'.

SMALLEST HORSE

The smallest horse in the world is Black Beauty, a black mare standing 47cm (18¾in) tall and weighing just 18.8kg (41½lb). The tiny horse was foaled in 1997 and is owned by Donald Burleson from Kittrell, North Carolina, USA.

CHAMPION THE WONDER HORSE

First broadcast from 1955 to 1956, *Champion the Wonder Horse* (*The Adventures of Champion*) was a children's television series set in the American West of the 1880s that chronicled the adventures of 12-year-old Ricky, his faithful dog Rebel and, of course, Champion. The horse was owned by producer Gene Autry, whose film, radio and television career as the Singing Cowboy was inextricably bound to that of Champion in his various incarnations.

Original Champion First appeared on screen in Melody Trail in 1935.

Champion Jr Appeared in Autry's films until 1950. More highly trained than Original Champion, he was billed as 'The Wonder Horse of the West' and 'The World's Wonder Horse'.

Television Champion Co-starred in Autry's last films and appeared on television in *The Gene Autry Show* and *The Adventures of Champion* in the 1950s.

Little Champ Trick pony that appeared in three Autry films and also made personal appearances in the 1940s.

Lindy Champion Tennessee Walking Horse that made aviation history in 1940 as the first horse to be flown from California to New York, when rushing from a movie set to his annual personal appearance at the World's Championship Rodeo in Madison Square Garden.

Touring Champion Another personal appearance horse, this one toured England in 1953. His hoofprints appear next to Autry's handprints at Grauman's Chinese Theater in Hollywood.

Champion Three Made personal appearances until 1960, when he retired to Autry's Melody Ranch in Newhall, California. He died in 1990: his reputed birth date of 1949 makes him a venerable Champion indeed.

JOUSTING POINTS

From the 11th century, jousting developed from free-for-all, deadly mêlées between an unlimited number of knights on horseback, to one-on-one organized tournaments for which, by the 15th century, scoring was reasonably standardized and would have looked something like this:

ACTION	POINTS
Unhorsing opponent with a lance break	3
Causing opponent to drop lance because of lance blow	3
Breaking lance by hitting tip of opponent's lance	3
Breaking lance at the base	2
Breaking lance between saddle and helm	1
Breaking lance on hitting saddle	-1
Failure to present self as target (horse swerves, etc)	-1
Hitting tilt* once with lance	-2
Hitting tilt* twice with lance	-3
Breaking lance within one foot of tip	0
Striking a horse with lance	Disqualification
Striking a man whose back is turned	Disqualification
Hitting tilt* three times	Disqualification

* A wooden fence running down the middle of the list (field on which the joust took place) to divide opponents from each other.

THE AMAZING SPINNING MACHINE

In 1885 'Professor' Sample arrived in London, bringing with him his 'Marvellous Horse Taming Machine' which, he claimed, could tame three or four wild horses per hour. This was achieved by securing the horse on the platform of the machine, which was then rotated rapidly by a steam engine until the horse was dizzy. Unfortunately (for the 'Professor'), the machine failed to work during several theatre performances – it was designed to function on a level surface and theatre stages are generally angled slightly towards the audience. Fortunately (for horses), the failure of this 'training system' allowed the invention to slip into obscurity.

Note This failure did not deter the 'Professor', who took on and won a horse-taming challenge with 'Leon the Celebrated Mexican Horse-Tamer' – an ex-pupil of Sample's and, in reality, an Australian printer's clerk named Franklin. It was later discovered that the result had been rigged.

RUMOURED TO BE LAW
In Raton, New Mexico, it is illegal for a woman to ride horseback down a public street wearing a kimono.

NEWMARKET STRIPES

In 1805, Oxfordshire blanket manufacturers Early's of Witney (established in 1669) received the exclusive contract to provide the London-based Hudson's Bay Company with blankets for the North American frontier trade. These were 'point' blankets: full or half stripes (points) were added to the blankets to indicate their size and trade value, each full point being the equivalent of one beaver pelt. All other trades were based on this standard. Today, the Witney* blanket is a traditional pure wool blanket placed under the rugs of stabled horses, and is usually golden yellow with black and red stripes. The blankets are perhaps more commonly known as Newmarket blankets, as their use is widespread among the racing fraternity.

* The last woollen mill in Witney closed in 2002 and the blankets are now produced in Derbyshire.

RIDE OR DRIVE?

From an archaeological site known as Dereivka, in present-day Ukraine, comes evidence dating back 6,000 years of a stallion with wear marks on its teeth that were almost certainly caused by the horse wearing a bit. This is 500 years before the earliest known wheel made its appearance, suggesting that horses were ridden before they were driven.

HORSEPOWER

'Horsepower' is a unit of power in the English system of units. The term was first coined by James Watt (1736–1819) to help market his improved steam engine intended to replace horses in coal mines. From the size of mill wheel used in a mine and the force with which he judged a horse could pull, Watt calculated:

1 horsepower (hp) = 33,000 foot-pounds per minute
(550 foot-pounds per second) = 745.69987158227022 watts (W)

This is usually rounded up to 1hp = 746W. Those familiar with horses may think Watt was somewhat optimistic in his calculation of their capabilities – or perhaps he intended to underpromise and overdeliver with his steam engine. Either way, comparison to a horse proved to be an enduring marketing ploy.

A MEMORY AID TO HORSEPOWER
In fourteen hundred and ninety-two
Columbus sailed the ocean blue
Divide that son-of-a-gun by two
And that's how many watts there are in a horsepower.

PALIO DI SIENA

Twice a year (2 July and 16 August) the *contrade* (districts) of Siena, Tuscany, hold a bareback horse race around the town square in honour of the Virgin Mary. Trials are held just before the race to accustom the horses (drawn by lot) to the jockeys, the track and the start, in which nine horses enter between the ropes and the tenth makes a running start.

On the day of the race, each horse is blessed in the chapel of its *contrada*. Preceded by a spectacular pageant commemorating Siena's struggles against its rival Florence, the race consists of three laps of the Piazzo del Campo. Riders are allowed to use their whips not only for their own horse, but also to distract other horses and riders. The winner is the first horse to cross the finish with its head decorations intact – the rider does not necessarily have to finish, and often does not.

BETTING FOLKLORE

* Avoid placing a wager on a horse that has had its name changed.

* Betting on the horse that has travelled furthest to the race will increase your chances of success.

* If you cannot see an obvious choice, make your selection by closing your eyes and sticking a pin in the list – but the pin must be from a bride's wedding dress.

WHITE HORSES AROUND THE WORLD

A few white horse depictions have appeared in countries outside the UK, based on the chalk cuttings found in southern England.

Name of white horse	Location	Date	Type	Comments
Bloemfontein	Free State, South Africa	After 1900	Painted rocks	This horse was built by British troops during the Anglo-Boer war (1899–1902), probably by men of the 2nd Battalion of the Duke of Edinburgh's Wiltshire regiment, so could be said to be the only Wiltshire white horse not in that county.
Ciudad Juárez	Chihuahua, Mexico	1980s	Painted	Created as a problem-solving exercise by architect Hector García Acosta and his son Carlos using 11,800 litres (2,600 gallons) of whitewash, this is a huge reproduction of the Uffington horse in Wiltshire, but facing left. The horse is over 750m (½ mile) long, and took three years to complete.
Waimate	South Island, New Zealand	Late 1960s	Concrete slabs	Constructed from 1,000 slabs with a pre-cast head weighing 2½ tonnes, almost single-handedly by Norman Hayman with some help from his wife Betty.

TERRITORY OR HAREM?

Two types of social organization occur in today's equines: solitary and territorial, and harems (herds) that move to grazing.

Territorial Grevy's zebra (*Equus grevyi*) and the African wild ass (*E. asinus*). A stallion may hold and defend the same territory for years, and when a mare strays into it he will mate with her unchallenged by other stallions. The only social bonds are between a mare and her foal.

Harems Plains zebra (*E. burchelli*) and mountain zebra (*E. zebra*), horses and ponies (*E. caballus*). A stallion will generally fight with others that display sexual behaviour towards his harem. Mating is determined by social structure, not territory. The instinct to bond holds the harem (a stallion, mares and their immature offspring) together, and is an important factor used to advantage in human training of these equines.

RODEO

SUPERSTITION

Always shave before the competition.
A rider should clean himself up for Lady Luck.

RUMOURED TO BE LAW

An ordinance in Wolf Point, Montana, states that: 'No horse shall be allowed in public without its owner wearing a halter.'

THE INCOMPARABLE RED RUM

* Bred in Ireland by Martyn McEnery to be a sprinter, sired by Quorum (selected simply because friends of the family owned the sire) out of a temperamental mare called Mared.

* The name Red Rum was derived from those of his dam and sire: Ma-red and Quo-rum.

* Sold for just 400 guineas as a yearling.

* Ran his first race (a two-year-old seller) appropriately at Aintree, dead-heating for first place with another McEnery horse, Curlicue.

* On the flat, Red Rum was ridden by eight different jockeys; over obstacles, he was ridden by 13, including a different one on each of his first six runs.

* Diagnosed as suffering from pedalostitis, a debilitating bone disease that can cripple horses.

* Bought by Southport trainer Donald 'Ginger' McCain for 6,000 guineas for owner Noel le Mare – McCain had never before paid more than 1,000 guineas for a horse.

* Trained by McCain on the local beach, which proved effective in curing the horse's bone problems.

* Won his first five races and started joint favourite for the 1973 Grand National, in which he overhauled front-runner Crisp (who was 15 lengths clear at the last) on the run-in to win by three-quarters of a length.

* Red Rum's time of 9 minutes 1.9 seconds set a new record, 20 seconds faster than the previous best mark, which would stand for 16 years.

* Won the Grand National again in 1974, and the Scottish Grand National three weeks later – a statue of the horse at Ayr racecourse marks the feat.

* Finished second in the Grand Nationals of 1975 and 1976.

* Won his third Grand National in 1977 at the age of 12 years.

* Retired the day before the 1978 Grand National (in which he would have run) following a hairline fracture.

* Died in 1995 at the age of 30 and was buried by the winning post on the Grand National course. A life-size bronze statue was erected at the course.

A HERCULEAN LABOUR

When mythological hero Hercules killed his wife and children in a fit of madness, his penance included 12 'Labours' under the direction of his cousin Eurystheus. The fifth of these was to clean up King Augeas' stables, which housed huge herds of cattle, goats and horses – in a single day. Hercules told King Augeas he would indeed clean out the stables in one day if Augeas would give him a tenth of his beasts, and the king agreed.

Hercules tore large openings in opposite sides of the yard that contained the stables, then dug trenches to two rivers that flowed nearby and turned the course of the rivers into the yard. The water rushed through the stables, flushing them out and removing the muck through the hole in the opposite wall.

Sadly for Hercules, when Augeas heard that Eurystheus was behind the task he refused to pay, and when Eurystheus heard that Hercules was to have been paid he refused to accept the Labour as complete. Elements of this myth may have resonance for those who work in stables today.

RUMOURED TO BE LAW

Pennsylvania law states: 'Any motorist who sights a team of horses coming toward him must pull off the road, cover his car with a blanket or canvas that blends with the countryside, and let the horses pass. If the horses appear skittish, the motorist must take his car apart, piece by piece, and hide it under the nearest bushes.'

SWEATY HORSES

* As 1 litre (1¾ pints) of sweat evaporates from a horse, about 580kcal of heat is lost.

* This is the amount of heat generated by 1–2 minutes of maximum sprint exercise, or 5–6 minutes of endurance exercise.

* In an 80km (50-mile) endurance ride a horse will lose 30–50kg (66–110lb) of body weight in water, primarily as sweat.

* A Standardbred will lose 5–15kg (11–38lb) of body weight during a 1-mile race, 90 per cent of which is water.

PONY GOAL

In polo, a 'pony goal' occurs when a pony causes the ball to go through the goal posts, usually by kicking it. Polo players take the view that this is natural for equine athletes, who enjoy the game as much as their riders. This type of goal counts and is always a real crowd-pleaser.

SOME GRAND NATIONAL LADY RIDERS

Year	Jockey	Horse	Placing	Comments
1977	Charlotte Brew	Barony Fort	Refused at fourth-last fence	First woman to ride in the race.
1982	Geraldine Rees	Cheers	8th and last	First woman to complete the course. In 1983 her mount Midday Welcome fell at the first fence.
1989	Venetia Williams	Marcolo	Fell at Becher's Brook	Retired after a fall two weeks later in which she broke her neck. Now a leading jump-race trainer.
1994	Rosemary Henderson	Fiddlers Pike	5th (only six finished)	Aged 51 (and a grandmother) when she rode in the race.
2005	Carrie Ford	Forest Gunner	5th	Winner of the Foxhunters' Chase (over the National fences) at Aintree in 2004 on the same horse, 10 weeks after giving birth to her daughter. Came out of retirement to ride.
2006	Nina Carberry	Forest Gunner	9th	Daughter of leading jockey Tommy and sister of Paul, who won the National in 1999 on Bobbyjo and fell at the 22nd fence in 2006.

POLO STOPPAGES

The game clock is stopped in the case of:

- A foul.
- Fallen pony or player.
- Pony or player injured.
- Broken tack.
- Loss of helmet.
- The ball rolling out of bounds.

A player may leave the field *without* the clock being stopped to:

- Change ponies, if the pony he is riding is not playing well but is not visibly injured.
- Replace a lost or broken mallet; alternatively, the player may simply reverse the mallet and strike the ball with the handle.

ST LEGER WINNER

Jockey Bill Scott won the St Leger a record nine times between 1821 and 1846.

REMEMBERING DRESSAGE MARKERS

To remember the order of letters around a 20 x 40m arena (A, K, E, H, C, M, B, F), try the following:

All King Edward's Horses Can Manage Big Fences
A Kindly Elephant Has Crushed My Blinking Foot!
A Fat Black Mother Cat Has Eight Kittens
All Fat Boys Make Cute Husbands Except Kevin

-FIRST MELBOURNE CUP WINNER-

Archer, the winner of the first running of the Melbourne Cup in 1861, was reported to have been walked 850km (560 miles) from Nowra to Flemington to take part in what is now Australia's most famous race. The following year the horse won again, but his attempt at a third successive victory was thwarted when his owner's entry was delayed in the post. As a result, a number of other owners removed their horses from the race in a show of solidarity, leaving a field of just seven – the smallest in the history of the Cup. In 1984, the horse was immortalized in a film named, not surprisingly, *Archer*.

-PATO-

First recorded in 1610, since 1953 Pato has been the national game of Argentina. Early games used a live duck (*pato* in Spanish) inside a basket instead of a ball, and the playing 'field' often stretched between neighbouring ranches, with the winning team being the one that reached their own ranch house in possession of the duck. Banned at various times for its violence (not only to the duck – riders were often trampled or wounded in knife fights precipitated by the game's rivalry), Pato was finally regulated during the 1930s under a set of rules inspired by those of polo.

Modern Pato is played using a leather ball with six handles; riders on the two four-man teams must try to gain possession of the ball by wresting it from each other's grasp and score by throwing it through a vertical ring (in contrast to the horizontal ring of basketball).

GRAND NATIONAL TRIVIA

* 13 mares have won the Grand National, the most recent being Nickel Coin, the winner in 1951.

* Four horses have won the race at odds of 100/1: Tipperary Tim (1928), Gregalach (1929), Caughoo (1947) and Foinavon (1967).

* Voluptuary, bred by Queen Victoria, had reputedly never jumped a fence before winning the National in 1884.

* Mick Fitzgerald was overcome by his victory on Rough Quest in 1996, saying: 'I've never enjoyed twelve minutes as much before. Sex is an anticlimax after that!'

* Bruce Hobbs was the youngest jockey to win the National, on Battleship in 1938 at the age of 17. The oldest successful rider was 48-year-old Dick Saunders on Grittar in 1982. Tim Durant was the oldest jockey to complete the course, partnering Highlandie in 1968 at the age of 68.

* The 1991 winner Seagram boasted the same name as the race sponsors. They did not own the horse, but had apparently been asked if they wanted to purchase him some time before the race.

* In 1992 a general election was to be held in the UK – and the Grand National was won by Party Politics.

* In 1997 the 150th running of the race was postponed until the Monday due to a bomb scare. Won by Lord Gyllene, this running also marked Sir Peter O'Sullevan's 50th and final commentary on the race for the BBC.

* Irish father (trainer) and son (jockey) combinations won the race in 1998 (Tommy and Paul Carberry with Bobby Jo), and 2000 (Ted and Ruby Walsh with Papillon).

THE SPANISH RIDING SCHOOL – IN VIENNA?

This apparent contradiction is resolved as soon it is realized that this world-famous institution is named after the horses that perform there, not the location. In 1580, a stud was founded by Archduke Charles II to produce fine horses for the Austrian court. This was based in Lipizza (now Lipica) near Trieste, hence the name Lipizzaner for the breed of horses the Archduke established using largely Spanish (Andalucian) bloodlines. Moved more than once during times of war, and frequently threatened with extinction, the stud is now located in the village of Piber in the Styrian Mountains, while the magnificent Lipizzaner stallions perform their spectacular High School displays and 'airs above the ground' surrounded by the baroque glory of the Spanish Riding School – of Vienna.

EARLY GAIT

Mary Leakey's 1979 discovery in Tanzania of fossilized footprints of *Hipparion*, a horse ancestor from 3,500,000 years ago, provides some evidence that horses were originally naturally 'gaited'. Analysis of the footprints shows that the animals were travelling at around 15kmph (9mph) in a running walk.

RUMOURED TO BE LAW

In Marshalltown, Iowa, it is against the law for a horse to eat a fire hydrant.

HORSE BRASSES

Now collectible artefacts, the small brass plates known as horse brasses were originally attached to harnesses to ward off the attentions of witches and the evil eye. As evil was associated with darkness, light was the antidote and the classic ancient designs for horse brasses (circle, crescent, rays) were related to sun worship. Brasses in all kinds of design proliferated in the 19th century, when horses were in widespread use in agriculture and for transport, and their owners took huge pride in the turnout of their animals.

COWBOY WISDOM

Speak your mind, but ride a fast horse.

THE 'NEAR' SIDE

Why is the left side of a horse called the 'near' side (and the right, the 'off' side), no matter how far away it may be? The answer lies not in horsemanship but swordsmanship. Swords are traditionally worn on the left, since that makes it easier for a right-handed swordsman to pull the sword from its scabbard. With his sword on the left, the swordsman would need to mount his horse on its left, otherwise the sword will get in the way.

The practice dates back at least to the ancient Greek military expert Xenophon, who gave a detailed description of mounting from the left (albeit without a stirrup, which had yet to be invented) in his treatise *On Horsemanship* (c.350BCE). Tradition (and safety considerations – a horse trained to be mounted on the left may take exception to a rider who attempts to get on from the right) has ensured that the practice continues to this day.

HORSE SELLER'S TERMS

Easy to catch Very old.

Quiet Lame in both front legs.

Very quiet Lame in all four legs.

Dead quiet Just dead.

Good in traffic/bombproof Lame all round, deaf and blind.

To loving home only Expensive.

To competitive home only Very expensive.

To good home only Not for sale unless you can (1) pay three times what he is worth; (2) allow the current owner to tuck him into bed every night; (3) are willing to sign a ten-page legal document.

Must sell Husband and kids are leaving home.

All offers considered I am in traction for six months.

COWBOY WISDOM No matter where you ride to, that's where you are.